CW00545056

£5 Soc
Soc Soc
9/24

Managing the
University Curriculum

SRHE and Open University Press Imprint
General Editor: Heather Eggins

Current titles include:

Ronald Barnett: *Improving Higher Education*
Ronald Barnett: *Learning to Effect*
Ronald Barnett: *Limits of Competence*
Ronald Barnett: *The Idea of Higher Education*
Tony Becher: *Governments and Professional Education*
Robert Bell and Malcolm Tight: *Open Universities: A British Tradition?*
Hazel Bines and David Watson: *Developing Professional Education*
Jean Bocock and David Watson: *Managing the University Curriculum*
David Boud *et al.*: *Using Experience for Learning*
John Earwaker: *Helping and Supporting Students*
Roger Ellis: *Quality Assurance for University Teaching*
Gavin J. Fairbairn and Christopher Winch: *Reading, Writing and Reasoning: A Guide for Students*
Shirley Fisher: *Stress in Academic Life*
Diana Green: *What is Quality in Higher Education?*
Jill Johnes and Jim Taylor: *Performance Indicators in Higher Education*
Ian McNay: *Visions of Post-compulsory Education*
Robin Middlehurst: *Leading Academics*
Henry Miller: *Managing Change in Universities*
Jennifer Nias: *The Human Nature of Learning: Selections from the Work of M.L.J. Abercrombie*
Keith Noble: *Changing Doctoral Degrees*
Gillian Pascall and Roger Cox: *Women Returning to Higher Education*
Graham Peeke: *Mission and Change*
Moira Peelo: *Helping Students with Study Problems*
Kjell Raaheim *et al.*: *Helping Students to Learn*
Tom Schuller: *The Future of Higher Education*
Michael Shattock: *The UGC and the Management of British Universities*
Geoffrey Squires: *First Degree*
Ted Tapper and Brian Salter: *Oxford, Cambridge and the Changing Idea of the University*
Kim Thomas: *Gender and Subject in Higher Education*
Malcolm Tight: *Higher Education: A Part-time Perspective*
David Warner and Gordon Kelly: *Managing Educational Property*
David Warner and Charles Leonard: *The Income Generation Handbook*
Sue Wheeler and Jan Birtle: *A Handbook for Personal Tutors*
Thomas G. Whiston and Roger L. Geiger: *Research and Higher Education*
Gareth Williams: *Changing Patterns of Finance in Higher Education*
John Wyatt: *Commitment to Higher Education*

Managing the University Curriculum

Making Common Cause

Edited by
Jean Bocock
and David Watson

The Society for Research into Higher Education
& Open University Press

Published by SRHE and
Open University Press
Celtic Court
22 Ballmoor
Buckingham
MK18 1XW

and

1900 Frost Road, Suite 101
Bristol, PA 19007, USA

First Published 1994

Copyright © the editors and contributors 1994

All rights reserved. Except for the quotation of short passages for the purpose
of criticism and review, no part of this publication may be reproduced, stored
in a retrieval system, or transmitted, in any form or by any means, electronic,
mechanical, photocopying, recording or otherwise, without the prior written
permission of the publisher or a licence from the Copyright Licensing Agency
Limited. Details of such licences (for reprographic reproduction) may be
obtained from the Copyright Licensing Agency Ltd of 90 Tottenham Court
Road, London, W1P 9HE.

A catalogue record of this book is available from the British Library

ISBN   0 335 19339 0 (pb)   0 335 19340 4 (hb)

A Library of Congress Cataloging-in-Publication Data
number is available for this book

Typeset by Graphicraft Typesetters Ltd, Hong Kong
Printed in Great Britain by St Edmundsbury Press Ltd,
Bury St Edmunds, Suffolk

Contents

List of Contributors

Ronald Barnett, Reader in the Centre for Higher Education Studies at the Institute of Education, University of London. He is the author of *The Idea of Higher Education* (1991), *Learning to Effect* (1992) and *Improving Higher Education* (1992).

Jean Bocock, Co-director of a research project on Further and Higher Education partnerships based at the University of Leeds. Previously she was a lecturer at Brunel and Sheffield Universities, following which she became the Higher Education Secretary at NATFHE. Her research interests are in curriculum issues in post-compulsory education.

Mary N. Haslum, Reader and Head of Psychology at the University of the West of England. Her research interests include approaches to learning in higher education, and specific learning difficulties, particularly dyslexia.

Dai Hounsell, Director of the Centre for Teaching, Learning and Assessment at the University of Edinburgh. His publications include *How Students Learn, The Experience of Learning, What is Active Learning?* and *Essay-Writing for Active Learning.*

Roger King, Vice-Chancellor and Chief Executive of the University of Humberside. Previously he was a Principal Lecturer, then Head of Department of Behavioural Sciences at Huddersfield Polytechnic. His publications include *The Middle Class, Capital and Politics* and *The State in Modern Society: New Directions in Political Sociology.*

Robin Middlehurst, Assistant Director in the Division of Quality Enhancement of the Higher Education Quality Council. She has experience of teaching at all levels of education, and has worked in higher education since 1986. Her research interests, pursued at the University of Surrey and the Institute of Education are in leadership and management and their development in universities. She is the author of *Leading Academics* (1993).

Peter Scott, Professor of Education at the University of Leeds. He was Editor of *The Times Higher Education Supplement* from 1976 until 1992. Previously he was a leader writer on *The Times.* He is a member of the Academia Europaea and a Fellow of the Society for Research into Higher Education. Among his books are *Knowledge and Nation* (1990) and *The Crisis of the University* (1984).

David Watson, Director of the University of Brighton. He previously taught at Crewe and Alsager College of Higher Education and Oxford Polytechnic, and has published widely on the history of ideas and higher education policy. He is the author of *Margaret Fuller* (1988), *Managing the Modular Course* (1989), *Developing Professional Education* (with Hazel Bines, 1992), and *Arendt* (1992). He is a former member of the Council for National Academic Awards and the Polytechnics and Colleges Funding Council. He sits on the Higher Education Funding Council for England and chairs its Quality Assessment Committee.

Foreword

Dr Kenneth J.R. Edwards
Chairman, Committee of Vice-Chancellors and Principals of Universities, and Vice-Chancellor, University of Leicester.

Higher education in the UK has been in a condition of permanent change over the past quarter of a century. During this period we have experienced dramatic changes in the organization, the governance, the funding, and above all the expectations of the system. Over the long haul, however, the chief characteristic of change has been expansion: initially in response to the Robbins Report; a decade later through the invention of the Open University; and most recently as a result of the initiative of Margaret Thatcher's administration from the mid-1980s to encourage the system to at least double its Age Participation Rate (from approximately 14 per cent to the current figure of just over 30 per cent). This latest phase has differed from its predecessors by being achieved without significant new investment in institutions and through substantial reductions in the revenue made available by government for each student place.

Expansion has meant increased opportunity, and is broadly welcomed across the political spectrum and within the CVCP. Its potentially beneficial effects upon our economy and our cohesion as a society are widely acknowledged. Equally, whatever the difficulties about measuring the quality of student (and institutional) achievement, or of maintaining consistency of educational standards over time, there is overwhelming evidence that the pool of people with 'ability to benefit' has not yet been used up. Great strides have been made towards the gender-neutrality of higher education, and smaller but important improvements in recruitment from ethnic minorities, but much less progress in admitting students from working-class families.

The efforts of staff within the universities and colleges to meet the demands of expansion have been nothing short of heroic. Most also applaud the intentions of the policy. Yet simultaneously there has developed a powerful sense of loss, which goes well beyond misplaced nostalgia for a golden age. The authors of this book capture the excitement and the concerns (sometimes as strong as despair) in their sub-title, 'Making Common Cause'. There is a sense that the community at the heart of the university or college is under unprecedented strain, and in some cases has broken apart.

Running through this book is a collective argument: that through careful and imaginative attention to the management of the curriculum (along with all the things we would like governments, and others outside of the institutions to do) the academic community can be restored. This is a hopeful argument, and in present circumstances a practical and a welcome one. It is, of course, by no means proven, but it inspires us all to endeavour to prove the authors right.

Acknowledgements

In addition to the authors of this book the 'Managing the Curriculum Group' which devised and carried through the project included: Vice-Chancellors Clive Booth (Oxford Brookes), Keith Thompson (Staffordshire), Alfred Morris (West of England) and Michael Harrison (Wolverhampton); Union Official David Triesman (then of NATFHE, now of AUT); Peter Scott (then of the *THES*, now of the University of Leeds; and Robin Middlehurst (then of the Institute of Education, now of the Higher Education Quality Council). Their continuing support, and that of other contributors to this book is gratefully acknowledged.

At the conference on 'Managing the University Curriculum in the Year 2000' in October 1992 we were also given highly professional and effective assistance by five chairs of workshops – Graham Badley, Andrew Wilson, Jessica Claridge, Clive Colling, and Robin Middlehurst – and five expert rapporteurs – Anne Palmer, Nigel Nixon, Ronald Barnett, Philip Jones and Sylvia Wicks. Support for students to attend the conference came from the institutions represented on the group, and crucial financial support for the conference itself from NATFHE, the *THES* and CNAA. Again we express our gratitude.

Putting together a multi-author volume is an administrative task of surprising complexity and tension. We were kept calm and on track by superlative support from Shirley Lee of NATFHE and Maureen Barnard and Katy Hiles of the University of Brighton. Finally, we express particular thanks for support and encouragement to Jim Munnery, June Huntington, Betty Skolnick, and Sarah and Michael Watson.

Jean Bocock
David Watson

List of Abbreviations

APEL	Assessment of Prior Experiential Learning
API	Age Participation Index
AUT	Association of University Teachers
BTEC	Business and Technician Education Council
CATS	Credit Accumulation and Transfer System
CDP	Committee of Directors of Polytechnics
CNAA	Council for National Academic Awards
CVCP	Committee of Vice-Chancellors and Principals of Universities
DfE	Department for Education
EHE	Enterprise in Higher Education
FTE	Full Time Equivalent
GNVQ	General National Vocational Qualification
HE	Higher Education
HEC	Higher Education Corporation
HEFCE	Higher Education Funding Council for England
HEQC	Higher Education Quality Council
HMI	Her Majesty's Inspectorate
ISL	Independent Student Learning
IT	Information Technology
NAB	National Advisory Body for Public Sector Higher Education
NATFHE	National Association of Teachers in Further and Higher Education
NVQ	National Vocational Qualification
OU	Open University
PCFC	Polytechnics and Colleges Funding Council
SHEFC	Scottish Higher Education Funding Council
TEC	Training and Enterprise Council
TES	Times Educational Supplement
THES	Times Higher Education Supplement
TQM	Total Quality Management
UCAS	Universities and Colleges Admissions System
UFC	Universities Funding Council
UGC	University Grants Committee

Introduction

Jean Bocock and David Watson

The best account of the process leading up to this book comes from one of the key participants, Clive Booth, Vice-Chancellor of Oxford Brookes University (then the Oxford Polytechnic):

> The chain of events began early in 1990. *The Independent* newspaper asked if a trainee journalist could spend a few days in Oxford Polytechnic, 'absorbing the atmosphere'. The Polytechnic readily consented. It was a decision we were to regret, for not long afterwards, an article appeared in *The Independent* about overcrowding and the pressures caused by rapid growth in student numbers at Oxford Polytechnic. It was topped off by a picture of students sitting in our grassy quadrangle, as they are prone to do when the sun shines, although the reader may well have gained the impression that there was insufficient room for them inside!
>
> On the whole it was a fair article and we could not seriously find much to complain about in it. It even included some valiant remarks from members of staff to the effect that, in spite of all the pressures, we were winning through and standards were being maintained.[1]
>
> This was too much for one of my academic colleagues, a long-time advocate for all that was best in the golden age. His letter to the Editor of *The Independent* appeared a few days after the article. It described the extra teaching hours he was working in order to cling to the small group sizes which he regarded as being so vital to the quality of higher education. And he went on vehemently to deny that we were achieving expansion while maintaining quality.
>
> At the time, the polytechnics and colleges nationally were in the midst of a dispute with lecturing staff over pay and conditions. I remember having a chance conversation with a senior union officer about the Polytechnic's recent adverse publicity. I said we accepted that we were a prime example of how barely tolerable stresses were being applied to the system. However, we had also been making extra

efforts to accommodate to change by using the innovatory ideas proposed by people like Graham Gibbs and his colleagues in our Educational Methods Unit.

The upshot of this conversation was that we should look for a new approach: instead of confronting one another in national disputes, no doubt to the delight of the Government, institutional leaders on the one hand and staff and their union on the other should try to do something more constructive. It was unrealistic to expect to be able to turn back the tide of change although we might succeed in channelling it in more sensible directions. Should we not try to come together to explore how we could take advantage of change for the benefit of the students, the staff and the institutions?

Although the fastest expansion had taken place in the polytechnics and colleges, it seemed clear that the creation of a single sector of higher education, with a strongly expansion-oriented formula for funding teaching, was going to expose both sides of the binary line to the same pressures. There could hardly be a better time for the old and new universities to find common cause.

The outcome was a conference on 'Managing the University Curriculum in the Year 2000' held in London in October 1992.

The conference

A small steering group (see Acknowledgements) attempted to draw together a broad cross-section of people involved in higher education to talk about the university curriculum. The organizers took great trouble to assemble a group balanced as far as possible by gender, subject discipline, staff grade and type of institution. In addition, students were invited to take a full part in the debate. In the event, 70 participants were organized into five groups, each with a chair and a rapporteur. The groups were constructed as far as was possible to ensure a spread of interests and backgrounds; each had at least one head of an institution, lecturer, member of support staff and student. The resulting dialogue was intense, occasionally frustrating and necessarily provisional in its conclusions. There was, however, little dissent about the importance and validity of the objective, of 'recovering a sense of common purpose'.

The workshop participants were provided with the following framework for discussion:

- What developments are inevitable?
- What developments are desirable?
- How do we prepare for these?
- What are your recommendations for action?

There were no formal outcomes, although some themes were recapitulated in a plenary session and a record subsequently circulated to participants.

The account in this introduction relies on that record, but also tries to draw together main threads under two headings, referring to the curriculum itself and the institutions within and by which it will be delivered.

Organizing the curriculum

> Higher education is characterized by intellectual affinity; organizing principles which ignore this are unlikely to be successful.

This aphorism, offered by one of the workshops as best encapsulating the problems the conference was trying to address, establishes a point of departure for exploration of the curriculum issues.

Not surprisingly, consensus was highest on the identification of 'inevitability' and least in evidence on 'action' points. Most changes identified were thought to be the inevitable consequence of increased access to the higher education system. Credit accumulation and transfer schemes and modular courses were widespread in the experience of participants, who also reported on moves to increase 'student-centred' learning (although warnings were entered about the need to separate rhetoric from reality in this area).

Exploring the forces shaping the curriculum (directly and indirectly) exposed a range of tensions, often reflecting the differing interests of managers, staff and students. It was recognized that argument about the curriculum and its organization is not just about designing the core 'product' of the university, but touches upon deeply-rooted educational values. The classic example is the defence by some of the 'traditional' universities of the three- or four-year single honours degree. Participants identifying this as constituting the 'gold standard' were clear in their assumption that as such it incorporated their key academic and professional values. These values embody a view of the curriculum as requiring sustained intellectual commitment as well as ensuring the initiation of students into a particular disciplinary or professional world. Traditional values were also widely recognized as being under threat. Student-centred learning was perceived by some as diminishing academic autonomy in decisions about curriculum content, design and delivery. For the traditional university the curriculum was presented as the outward expression of accumulated private worlds of academic knowledge, mediated and given coherence by subject groupings and departments. As such it was regarded as one of the key institutional expressions of the 'intimacy' referred to in Chapter 2.

Motives and incentives for changing the shape and nature of the curriculum were largely seen as lying with managers, under organizational and financial pressure from the funding councils, although there was some recognition of legitimately changing expectations of groups of actual and potential 'consumers' (the students). A recurring call was for a greater sense of 'ownership' rather than 'imposition' of change. The dilemma was couched in terms of finding a form of curriculum organization which acknowledges the greater diversity of legitimate interests in it without undermining the values which have given it its historical and current strength. The micro-political realities of patterns of collusion were exposed: managers with students (and against staff) in favour of greater freedom and flexibility; staff with students (and against managers) in responding to pressures like overcrowding, decreased access to tutors and the like.

A major consequence of these changes seemed to be not only declining autonomy, but also a declining sense of responsibility. Teaching staff felt particularly acutely a sense of being in the front line of the battle resulting from institutional changes which they had neither chosen nor willed. Rising expectations on the part of students (and others) could lead to unmet expectations and academics easily become the focal point for the resulting frustrations. They can also fuel the flames, as the managers pointed out.

This is not to say that some participants (perhaps a majority) did not find some stimuli for changing the curriculum that were positive and potentially liberating. Almost all, however, referred to the by-product of a sharp decline in academic morale, which was thought to be endemic and an impediment to constructive change. The two elements of the system most in need of attention if this decline were to be arrested (and even reversed) were internal communications and staff development.

The increasing diversity of roles and responsibilities required of academic staff was also an issue of concern. The various shifts, in particular away from the heartland of 'subject' expertise, were seen as undermining a sense of professional competence, without training or development to support new or changing roles.

In summary, the vision of the future was one in which the organization of the curriculum would become more complex and problematic rather than less; that more external bodies would impose their interests; that stakeholders other than the academic staff would influence its definition; and that fundamental traditional values would thereby be challenged. Two needs were strongly expressed in the face of this transformation: first that academic integrity and coherence should not only be redefined but also positively reasserted; and secondly, that several influential parties should be more modest in their advocacy of change.

Organizing the university

Perhaps understandably, participants in the workshops had equally strong but less precise views about necessary and desirable changes in the organization of their institutions to meet the changing circumstances of the curriculum. It was also in these parts of the dialogue that lines tended to be drawn more emphatically between groups with differing responsibilities and perspectives. As a consequence the temperature rose.

Excitement was, we feel, genuinely shared about the prospects for a more open, accessible system in meeting goals of a more inclusive and civilized society, as well as a more productive economy. None of the participants subscribed to the interpretation that (following the Robbins principle) the pool of people with ability to benefit from higher education had been used up, or was even close to being used up. On the other hand, there was a clear sense of the fragility of the institutional cultures which had reacted heroically to meeting these demands. Part of the mood of these discussions was encapsulated in a poster stuck to the wall by one group. It read simply: 'Enormity of task – Scarcity of resource.'

A consistent influence on both mood and substance of the discussion was the perception of externally driven change, the implications of which were inadequately analysed and 'managed' within the institutions. Speed of change was also seen as being at least as damaging as its direction (which, as indicated above, could often be welcomed). There was a sense that good ideas have been extrapolated beyond what is sensible; that 'managers' have succumbed to a frenzy of change – starting new things before their bases are secure or even finished; that the roots are being pulled up to see how the plant is growing.

Much of this frustration and latent tension led to another feature of the dialogue. We had several examples in action of the 'asymmetrical sympathy syndrome' defined by David Watson in Chapter 5. It is no accident that much of the time and energy was spent on trying to get beyond stereotyping, to understand more fully the objectives and motives of others. It was also predictable that the central theme in institutional terms was power.

No list of recommendations or points for action can afford to ignore this important backdrop. Two important dimensions of power are potentially separable. First we need, within the institutions, a clear, cold-eyed analysis of how much and what type of power (perhaps best defined here as the ability to take independent action, and to require others to cooperate in its execution) is granted to institutions, and how they are held responsible for their use of it. The second is, of course, how that power and responsibility is distributed within the organization. In the past lack of clarity on these points was not necessarily a bad thing, as it enabled individuals and groups to range widely and creatively across the institution, only meeting resistance *in extremis*. The external imperatives covered by this volume make continuation of that assumption difficult if not dangerous. We reached no firm conclusions, but perhaps by the end we understood each other a little better.

Recommendations

Beyond this overriding therapeutic need there were some constructive recommendations for change. These focused on four main areas:

Communications

This was a leitmotif of the whole day. Objectives about mutual understanding and mutual respect were seen to stand or fall on the ability of institutions to establish and maintain open and complete systems of communications. One group put the point like this: 'open and democratic communication systems, encompassing all members of the institution needed to be in place as a prerequisite for all other developments'.

Teamwork

Secondly, there was consensus that new curricular models needed new working arrangements for the team delivery of that curriculum. It was also recognized that this possibility might corrode the traditional self-image of the university lecturer. On the downside for academics would be the loss of exclusive rights over the design and delivery of courses. The roles of other staff in supporting learning would need to be developed and recognized, including librarians, technicians, computing officers, counsellors (of all types) and even administrators. On the upside, the prospect of better professional support was recognized, including the potentially liberating effects of more precise definition of roles. Above all, the case for mutual respect was underlined.

Staff development

Such shifts in role could not be accepted or sustained without the appropriate professional development of staff. This should have several dimensions; to assist teachers systematically with teaching, and managers with managing!

Values

Deep down, of course, these modifications are heavily value-laden, and all about institutional cultures. More humility about whom the institutions really existed to serve was urged, especially in terms of curriculum development. One group attempted to approach the question of differential roles by 'examining the entitlement of students'. Their conclusion was stark: 'No progress was made, but there was agreement that the institutions were not managing the expectations of students very well.'

Since the conference in 1992 a number of things have changed. Government has had second thoughts about the expansion that has doubled participation (from about 14 per cent to about 30 per cent of each age cohort) in less than a decade, and the debate about quality has moved on to a new plane as this aspect of the Further and Higher Education Act of 1992 bites, subjecting institutions on both sides of the former binary line to 'audit' by the Higher Education Quality Council and 'assessment' by the Funding Councils. Above all there is deepening concern about the quality of life of all who work in the institutions – students and all types of staff. The following chapters, which have been developed out of, and sometimes well beyond, the conference, attempt to set this context, elaborate on the concerns and interests of all of the stakeholders (inside and outside the institutions), and suggest practical ways in which some of these concerns can be met. As our title suggests, the key dilemma is how to recover and nurture a shared sense of purpose between those who manage and those who deliver a curriculum which is itself under social and economic pressure.

Overview

This book is divided into four parts, the first of which deals with the background of the changes taking place in UK universities and the likely impact on their organization.

In Chapter 1, Peter Scott and David Watson examine the transformations currently taking place in universities, locating them in the context of higher education development since the late 1970s. Four major areas of change are explored (the end of the binary system, expansion, and new patterns of funding, both for teaching and student support), providing the backdrop for consideration of their implications for management of the university curriculum. It is argued that a lower-cost, higher-volume system of education provision can be achieved without compromising standards, but that the university curriculum must be more purposefully managed for this to happen.

Chapter 2 develops this argument, proposing closer association between management and teaching. Scott and Watson move on to explore the question of whether wider access to university and the introduction of tighter efficiency controls are compatible with the tradition of academic and pastoral intimacy within UK universities.

In Chapter 3, Robin Middlehurst and Ron Barnett point out that the changes occurring in higher education are largely driven by external forces, such as Britain's economic decline and the increasing influence of information technology. It is argued that these influences are forcing higher education curricula out of their traditional base disciplines. As a result, the boundaries between traditionally separate subject areas, 'the academic heartland of universities', are becoming blurred, with many academics losing their sense of professional identity and autonomy. Middlehurst and Barnett warn of the dangers of poorly managed change, and emphasize the importance of good communication between managers and academic staff, proposing a four-cornered strategy for approaching changes to the university curriculum.

In Part 2, issues in the management of universities are explored from the perspectives of two institutional heads.

Roger King (Chapter 4) argues that a new 'compact' must be reached between managers and staff, adapting to the new market-orientated concepts of education as product and students as consumers. The traditional academic collegial forum, he says, is no place for planning product development strategies. Such activity must have a managerial focus, which will lead institutional managers to the heart of the academic domain. He argues for increased emphasis on human resource policies, facilitating the redefinition of staff roles in the process of adapting to new requirements.

David Watson's Chapter 5 highlights the contradictory demands being faced by institutional heads in the changing world of higher education. Writing as Director of one of the 'new' universities, Watson reveals the complexities embodied in the concept of the 'higher education corporation' before moving on to an exploration of the myths generated within higher education over the years, the persistence of which continue to impede progress. The ambiguities thriving in changing universities generate daily dilemmas for their managers who must continually balance legitimate but conflicting pressures.

Part 3 shifts the perspective to that of middle managers and lecturers, covering the basic realities of adaptation in the changing world of higher education.

In Chapter 6, Dai Hounsell considers teaching quality in relation to curriculum support. In arguing that universities of the future must develop distinctive strengths in order to compete in a complex 'marketplace', he explores three areas of educational development with profound implications for curriculum content and management: resources; teaching–learning strategies; and accountability.

In Chapter 7, Mary Haslum provides a personal 'Course Leader's Perspective' on modularization at the University of the West of England. Haslum covers the recurrent themes of wider access to higher education, increasing student choice, increasing student numbers and teaching quality. The emphasis is on the hidden costs of such dramatic changes, especially those which have to be met by the staff at ground level, 'who drive the system and deliver the courses'.

Jean Bocock's Chapter 8 explains why so many academics feel threatened by the changes taking place in universities. Increased diversity within universities means a broadening of the responsibilities of lecturers, some of whom feel ill-equipped for the tasks they are now expected to perform. Bocock analyses the sense of 'academic devaluation' that many lecturers are experiencing, due to a perceived 'erosion of professional autonomy', and a pervasive sense of loss. Bocock argues that in order for the curriculum to be managed effectively, lecturers must redefine their roles and achieve a balance between their own values and aspirations and those of the institutions within which they work.

Part 4 concludes the book with a chapter looking to the future. In Chapter 9, Bocock and Watson analyse the prospects for renewal of professional identities and professional roles and offer a guardedly optimistic prognosis.

Note

1. MacDonald, M. The poly that's pushed to the limit, *The Independent*, 3 May 1990.

Part 1

The Changing Context

1

Setting the Scene

Peter Scott and David Watson

Higher education in the UK is in the middle of a turbulent but exhilarating period of growth, in size and scope, which can reasonably be compared to the Robbins–Crosland era a generation ago when the new universities such as Sussex and Warwick were established, the colleges of advanced technology promoted to university status and the polytechnics first planned. As in the mid-1960s the landscape of higher education is being transformed in the early 1990s. The binary structure established in the 1960s, with autonomous (and élite?) universities neatly balanced by local authority maintained (and mass?) polytechnics, has been abandoned. Rapid expansion of student numbers has resumed after the pause of the early and mid-1980s, at any rate in the former university sector. Productivity gains, efficiency measures and 'market' elements have been built into funding systems. Financial support for students has been reformed – and reduced.

All these policies have had a powerful if indirect influence on the shape, and so the management, of the university curriculum. The abandonment of the binary system has disrupted sectoral demarcations and, arguably, disturbed institutional identities and missions. Expansion has sucked new kinds of student into higher education with different expectations and ambitions from those of well-qualified (and well-drilled) school-leavers. Budgetary constraints have forced institutions to re-examine curricular practices (such as labour-intensive small-group teaching) and professional routines (such as defined teaching loads and a restricted academic year) which appear to be inefficient. In addition, attempts to introduce 'market' mechanisms into funding systems, although ineffective in their technical details, have produced a more consumerist orientation; students are now seen as customers who must be wooed. Finally, the inadequacy of student support has obliged institutions to reshape their courses, acknowledging that most students work in their vacations or that part-time study must be combined with full-time work. In each case, and cumulatively, the curriculum has had to be revised in the light of these changing circumstances.

In addition, of course, direct reforms of the university curriculum have been undertaken. The knowledge and skills-content of particular courses have been subject to remorseless obsolescence and renewal. This is not a new phenomenon. It was noted by Martin Trow in the 1970s when he remarked on the contrast between the university's structural immobility, or at any rate conservatism, in what he termed its 'public world', and the university's intellectual dynamism in the 'private world' of research-led disciplines (Trow 1973). Not everyone, of course, has accepted that disciplines are dynamic; they detect powerful elements of continuity, conservatism and even complacency. However, the combined effect of two new factors has been to intensify the disciplinary dynamism highlighted by Trow while reducing the sharp contrast he draws between 'public' and 'private worlds' of higher education.

First, it has become difficult to dispute the radical effects on the university curriculum of the explosion of knowledge, and its increasingly rapid turnover, and the demand for ever more sophisticated skills, which too are prey to accelerating obsolescence. In a fast-changing post-industrial world the emphasis, not just in research but in teaching too, has tilted even more decisively towards adaptation and away from continuity. Secondly, these radical effects are now mirrored in reforms in the structure of the curriculum. These reforms have been introduced at every stage: at or before the point of entry as special access courses and franchising schemes have proliferated; in mid-course as modular degree schemes and credit accumulation and transfer systems have been widely introduced; and in the context of assessment and outcomes as course portfolios and student transcripts have become more popular.

The intention in this chapter is to explore the four broad trends – the end of the binary system, the resumption of rapid expansion, new funding systems and changing patterns of student support – which together establish the conditions and the context in which the university curriculum must be managed. These conditions and context form the subject of Chapter 2.

The end of the binary system

For at least a decade before the Further and Higher Education Act 1992 under which the binary system was finally abandoned, UK higher education had been on a convergent course. From the start, the binary system indicated only an approximate demarcation of missions between universities on the one hand and polytechnics and colleges of higher education on the other. Despite attempts to construct an 'alternative' polytechnic philosophy of higher education (Robinson 1968; Birch 1988), the real binary demarcation was administrative rather than academic (Scott 1993). The key distinction between universities and polytechnics was summed up in the phrase used to describe the latter, 'the public sector', which located binary differences in Trow's 'public' rather than 'private world'. Only in the loosest sense could the polytechnics and colleges ever be regarded as even approximating to the 'mass' component of UK higher education and the universities to the 'élite' component.

Unlike in many states in the USA no attempt was made to impose a rigid academic hierarchy, with most institutions confined to offering undergraduate and taught postgraduate courses and only élite universities permitted to provide doctoral and post-doctoral level qualifications and to engage in substantial research. Under the auspices of the Council for National Academic Awards (CNAA) the polytechnics were always able to offer the same academic qualifications as universities up to and including PhD. Nor were the polytechnics in England and Wales restricted to providing narrowly defined professional and vocational education like the German *Fachhochschulen* or the Dutch higher professional schools, although efforts were made in Scotland to distinguish more clearly between the roles of the universities and of the Central Institutions. Most subjects were offered on both sides of the binary line; the only prominent exception was (and is) Medicine and certain allied subjects which remain a university monopoly. Indeed, in the 1970s and 1980s the growth in the number of polytechnic and college students was most rapid in Business, Management, Applied Social Studies and Humanities rather than in Science, Engineering and Technology, the bed-rock subjects of advanced further education in the 1960s.

From the late1970s, the administrative demarcation between universities and polytechnics, the heart of the binary system, began to be eroded. The need to create a national planning framework for the polytechnics and, by implication, to coordinate their development with that of the universities (no longer regarded as beyond the reach and responsibility of the Department of Education and Science) had come to be widely accepted. The establishment of the National Advisory Body (NAB) in 1982, after the first and failed attempt to break the links between local education authorities and polytechnics and colleges, provided such a framework. The NAB also quickly engaged in vigorous dialogue with the University Grants Committee (UGC) on a growing number of matters of mutual transbinary interest, so creating a context in which coordination became possible. During the 1980s the polytechnics and colleges quickly came to be regarded as a parallel rather than subordinate sector of higher education. When, at the second attempt, they were finally removed from local authority control by the Education Reform Act of 1988, the already powerful momentum towards convergence between the two sectors was further increased. Although two separate agencies were established, the Universities Funding Council (UFC) in succession to the UGC and the Polytechnics and Colleges Funding Council (PCFC) in succession to the NAB, it was clear to many people that there were now in the UK two parallel 'national' systems of higher education which seemed predestined to merge. Increasingly, policy issues arose which concerned the system as a whole rather than its separate sectors. The administrative and political difficulties created by the painful transition from UGC to UFC threw in disarray the development of the universities, up to then the lead sector in higher education, while the PCFC built on the foundations laid by the NAB policies which did much to raise the institutional consciousness of the polytechnics and colleges. The result was a subtle but decisive shift in the balance of power within higher education.

Few people may have anticipated the speed with which unification was finally achieved with the passage of the Further and Higher Education Act in 1992. But, although events in high politics accelerated the erosion of the binary system, the abandonment of a demarcation which had lost much of its (predominantly administrative) rationale between 1977 and 1988 was already inevitable. In terms of planning and funding, the case for the abolition of the UFC and PCFC and their replacement by new bodies, the Higher Education Funding Councils (HEFC), was uncontestable. There was widespread and bipartisan support for the abandonment of the binary system. The polytechnics warmly welcomed this long-anticipated outcome; the colleges of higher education too, although they remain concerned about the role of smaller colleges in a unified system dominated by larger universities. University opinion acquiesced although wearily and without enthusiasm. The patterns of post-secondary education before 1988, between 1988 and 1992 and since 1992 are summarized in Figs 1.1–1.3.

The abandonment of the increasingly artificial *administrative* separation of higher education into two sectors, however, has not abolished at a stroke the (dwindling?) differences of ethos and mission between the traditional universities and former polytechnics nor undermined the arguments for and against a more refined division of *academic* labour. Yet in the context of managing the curriculum it is the latter considerations that carry most weight. Seen in this light the end of the binary system has asked as many questions as it has answered. The intentions that lay behind its abandonment and the desired outcomes of the new unified system are not clear, at whichever of the system's many levels they are examined – the Department for Education, the HEFCE (and the Scottish and Welsh funding councils) or among institutional managers, teachers and researchers. A number of questions, all of which are directly relevant to the future pattern of the university curriculum, remain difficult to answer.

First, is the ending of the binary system a vote of confidence in the former polytechnics (and, *sotto voce*, a vote of no confidence in the traditional universities), or final confirmation that, despite the brave efforts of the polytechnics to establish an alternative brand image, the 'university' has remained the only valid institutional currency in higher education? Secondly, is the outcome likely to be a reinterpretation of traditional notions of academic quality, the opening up of new and challenging democratic possibilities, or a levelling down of academic standards, the irreversible abandonment of the 'gold standard' of the honours degree? Thirdly, will the creation of a unified system lead to a 'New Deal' for the former polytechnics certainly and possibly the colleges of higher education, in terms of enhanced resources and more equitable funding, or will it accelerate the trend towards a much starker stratification between research universities

Figure 1.1   Post-secondary education in the UK (until 1988).

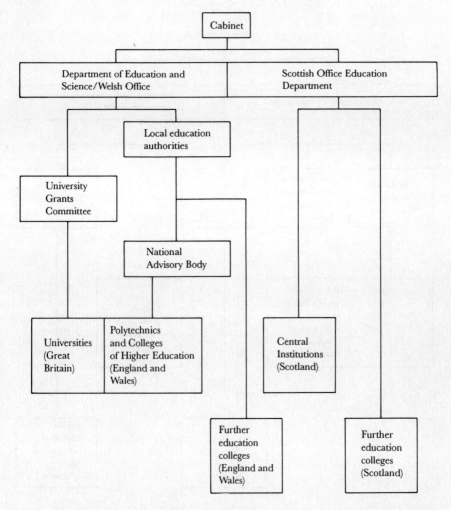

and mainly teaching institutions? If the first accounts in these sets of alternatives are preferred, a more open, flexible and imaginative curriculum is
likely to develop which will be common to most, if not all, university and
colleges; if the second are regarded as more plausible, the result could be
a dispersed and, in some cases, debased curriculum.

Lurking behind these three sets of alternatives is a simple but fundamental question. Institutionally and administratively the binary system may have
been finally abandoned, because the two sectors have been converging
for more than two decades. But academically or, better, normatively has
the binary system survived? Indeed has it been strengthened, because the

Figure 1.2   Post-secondary education in the UK (1988–92).

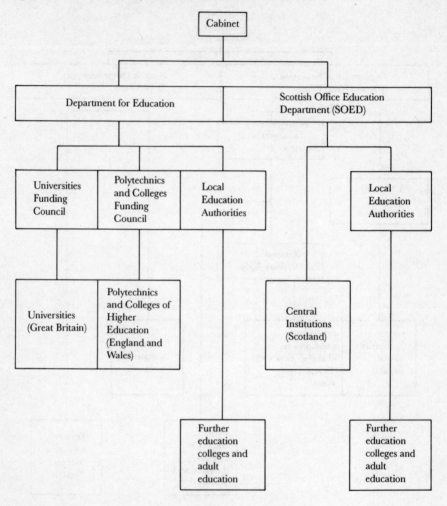

polytechnics since the early 1980s have established a more coherent and self-confident (and distinctive?) mission?

The growth of higher education

The scale of expansion

After the 1970s, a decade of stuttering growth, the 1980s witnessed a resumption of rapid expansion which recalled the impressive growth rates of the 1960s. At the start of the present decade there were 1.2 million students

Figure 1.3 Post-secondary education in the UK (since 1992).

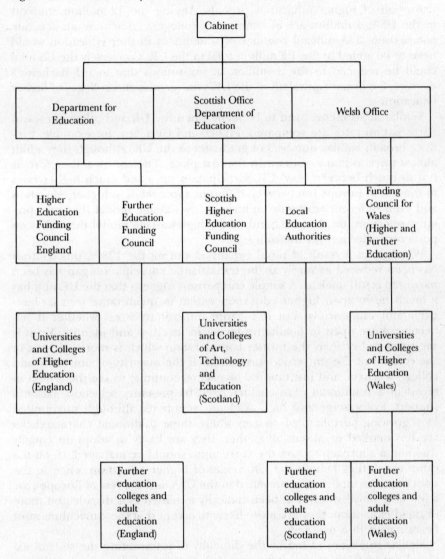

in universities and other colleges, an increase of 41 per cent since 1980. As a result, in the past 10–15 years, the UK has ceased to be an underdeveloped country in terms of post-school participation. Grossed up to reflect the 1:5 population differential between the UK and the USA, the present UK total translates into the US equivalent of 6 million students. There are more than 12 million students in US universities and colleges, which at first sight suggests that the UK participation rate is still only half of the rate in the USA. But on the other side of the Atlantic a much wider definition of higher education prevails. Among the 12 million students in the USA, 4 million are in community colleges. To achieve an accurate comparison, a significant number of students in further education would need to be added to the 1.2 million total in the UK. Conversely the US total could be reduced to the 8 million in institutions that award Bachelor's degrees, the broad equivalent of the UK's universities and colleges of higher education.

Similar adjustments need to be made when the UK and other European participation rates are compared. France and Germany, for example, produce broadly similar numbers of graduates as the UK, although they admit almost twice as many students in the first place. The contrast, therefore, is not so much between 'low' UK participation rates and much higher rates in the rest of Europe but between different approaches to higher education and even different academic cultures, a low-wastage model that uses pre-entry selection, on the one hand, and a high-wastage model that relies on post-entry selection on the other.

Whether, as a result of rapid expansion during the 1980s, this contrast has been reduced as surely as the transatlantic participation gap has been narrowed is still unclear. A simple comparison suggests that the UK now has a much more open higher education system in quantitative terms, objectively and numerically. But it is more difficult to assess whether it has become more open in qualitative terms, in its ethos and identity. Yet it is the latter rather than the former consideration which is more relevant in the context of the university curriculum. If the majority of university and college teachers, and institutional managers, continue to see the system in terms of a traditional core characterized by pre-entry selection, pastoral support, low wastage and high academic standards, although surrounded by a growing periphery of courses where these traditional characteristics are less marked or absent altogether, they are likely to adopt an equally traditional approach to how the curriculum should be managed. If, on the other hand, they believe the UK model of higher education, once so distinct from the models that prevailed in the USA and the rest of Europe (bar a few élite universities), has been radically modified by a decade and more of rapid expansion, they are more likely to accept that the curriculum must be managed in a new way.

Similar issues are raised by the difficulty of interpreting the shift in external perceptions of the university. If the growth of the past decade can be explained largely in terms of well-understood phenomena, such as the expansion of the middle class, the onward-and-upward march of credentialism or even the recession of the early 1990s, it is difficult to argue that any radical adjustment has taken place in the positioning of higher education within UK society. Rather, universities and colleges have merely responded to shifting social balances and changing economic circumstances. As a result, the pressure to transform higher education and, in particular the university curriculum, is likely to be limited.

But if the present expansion can only be explained in terms of a sea change in popular attitudes towards participation in higher education, in outcome if not intention, then a more radical repositioning of higher education is under way. The social purposes and so the academic values of the university need to be substantially modified. So too does the university curriculum. Certainly there have been dramatic improvements in the Age Participation Index (API), the proportion of young people going on to higher education. In 1970 it was fewer than 1 in 10; a decade later it was almost 1 in 5; the latest figure is 30 per cent and it is confidently predicted that the Government's target of 1 in 3 will be comfortably exceeded well before the end of the century. But translating such numerical indices into proof of a social revolution is difficult. Of course a simple either/or choice between these two interpretations cannot be made. There are familiar phenomena which nevertheless have radical social consequences; the most obvious is the changing role of women. However, some sense of the balance of probability between these two broad accounts of the causes and effects of expansion is needed to begin to understand its implications for the curriculum and how it should be managed. This is far from easy. The main engine of student growth during the past decade has been the increasing number of school-leavers with standard entry qualifications. The proportion with one or more A Level or Scottish Higher grade passes (or two or more AS Levels) grew from 16.5 per cent in 1980–1 to 23.2 per cent in 1990–1 in schools. If all young people studying for A Levels and their equivalents in further education are included, the proportion rose to 28 per cent in 1992–3 (DfE 1993a, b). A higher proportion of those with the necessary qualifications have chosen to go on to higher education. An important reason for these significantly higher qualification and willingness rates is that today's school-leavers are the children of those who benefited from the greatly expanded opportunities to enter higher education in the wake of the Robbins Report a generation ago. This generational pattern suggests that some slackening of demand is to be expected in the late 1990s and early years of the next century as the children of those who went to higher education during the slower-growth 1970s leave school. However, the pool of graduate parents will continue to grow so no serious setback is to be expected.

Particularly significant within this pattern of increased demand from school-leavers have been the growing aspirations of girls and the heightened aspirations of their parents. Nearly all the improvement in examination successes is accounted for by higher levels of achievement among girls. There was almost no improvement among boys during the 1980s. Little attempt has been made to explore this gender differential, despite its obvious relevance for the future of the university curriculum and its importance for assessing the wider significance of the social transformation of higher education. As a result, the proportion of women students increased from 36 to 45 per cent during the 1980s. If nursing and other paramedical students are included, their share is 49 per cent. Clearly, there will be less scope for future student growth to be fuelled by the equalization of participation rates between men and women. Nevertheless, the feminization of higher education, a global phenomenon but especially intense in the developed world, will have far-reaching implications.

For many, the expansion of higher education during the past decade has been a story of 'more of the same' (if, indeed, it is reasonable to regard increasing female participation in such a conventional light). Although the number of mature students has increased, many are still young adults, sometimes already qualified, who are better seen as deferred initial entrants rather than genuine second-chancers. Also the number of part-time students has grown more slowly than that of full-time students – by 113,000 between 1980–1 and 1989–90 compared with 162,000 extra full-time students. Even in the polytechnics, full-time student numbers rose by 47 per cent while part-time numbers increased by only 37 per cent (DfE 1993c). A possible explanation is the lack of any direct state support for fees. In addition the proportion of students on non-degree courses has also shrunk, although several of the former polytechnics now include in their mission statements a commitment to reversing this trend.

It may be incautious to conclude from the above that the expansion of the 1980s and early 1990s has been produced by the more intensive exploitation of traditional sources of likely students and, therefore, that UK higher education has yet to make a decisive breakthrough to wider participation. There are two reasons for doubting this interpretation. First, longer-run series of statistics stretching over two decades since 1970 suggest that the proportion of part-time students (although not of those on non-degree courses) has not declined but steadily increased, especially among women (Table 1.1). The number of part-time women students in the polytechnics and colleges of higher education rose by almost 800 per cent between 1970–1 and 1989–90 (DfE 1992). Of course, it can be argued that the trend towards part-time established in the 1970s was reversed during the 1980s, perhaps because the polytechnics raised their academic sights in their rivalry with the universities. A simpler interpretation, however, is that the shortage of full-time places, and the attempts by the universities to cut their intakes, temporarily distorted the balance between full-time and part-time provision in the polytechnics, although some of the smaller ones and some colleges of higher education were anxious to increase their core of full-time students.

Secondly, the expansion of higher education is not an isolated phenomenon. It is part of a much wider trend towards increased participation in all forms of post-secondary education. At the beginning of the 1980s, 52 per cent of 16–18-year-olds were still in school or at college; a decade later this proportion had risen to 60 per cent. The growth of student numbers in universities and colleges also has to be seen in the context of the changing labour market for young people. Higher levels of unemployment, which many commentators suspect are structural rather than cyclical, have encouraged many governments to reform traditional patterns of job training,

Table 1.1 Expansion of higher education in the UK by type of institution, sex and mode of attendance (1970–90).

Sex (PT/FT)	Universities			Polytechnics/CHEs			Open University		
	1970–71	1989–90	per cent	1970–71	1989–90	per cent	1970–71	1989–90	per cent
FT/men	167,000	200,000	20	107,000	170,000	59	–	–	–
FT/women	68,000	151,000	122	114,000	169,000	48	–	–	–
PT/men	18,000	31,000	72	110,000	159,000	45	14,000	47,000	236
PT/women	6,000	23,000	283	12,000	103,000	758	5,000	43,000	740

Source: *Education Statistics for the United Kingdom* (National Commission on Education)

both through direct intervention and by building partnerships between education and industry. The creation of Training and Enterprise Councils (TECs) is an example of the latter. As a result, there is a deep-rooted secular trend in most developed countries towards a lengthening of initial education and more-systematic training, of which the growth of mass higher education systems is a component. Both appear to be aspects of the development of a post-industrial society.

The shape of expansion

The overall scale of expansion is only one significant aspect. Almost as important is its shape, in particular the difference between growth rates in the old universities and the former polytechnics. In the former students grew by 22 per cent. Growth in the latter was more than three times as fast; the number of polytechnic students increased by 72 per cent. This differential was among the most significant phenomena of the 1980s. Not only did it radically readjust the balance between the two sectors, with the universities losing their previously unchallenged status as the majority (as well as the élite) sector of higher education in 1986, but it also made the abandonment of the binary system inevitable, such was the weight, political and academic, acquired by the polytechnics. Yet few people at the start of the 1980s could have predicted that growth in the universities would stagnate and expansion be concentrated instead in the polytechnics and also (although less dramatically) the colleges of higher education.

After the 1981 cuts, a 15 per cent reduction in the universities' recurrent grant, there was a momentary downturn. The UGC's instinct was to protect the unit of resource which had been steadily eroded over the past decade. It therefore ordered a 5 per cent cut in student numbers. Universities which recruited more than their allocated targets were 'fined'. In the outcome this conservative policy was quickly overwhelmed by events, not least the contrary example of the polytechnics. The polytechnics' commitment to expansion, therefore, arose partly by accident. During the 1970s the growth rates of the two sectors has been similar. They diverged after the 1981 cuts when students who could not find university places turned to the polytechnics. Subsequently, this expansionary policy was espoused, initially with reluctance, by the NAB established in 1982. Of course, the growth of student numbers in the polytechnics was not wholly an accident nor the outcome of external events (whether the UGC's shortsightedness or the creation of the NAB). It also reflected the broadening of their mission during the later 1970s and early 1980s, away from a narrow professional, even technological, interpretation of their role within higher education towards a much wider and inclusive vocationalism.

Expansion was also endorsed by the Government. At first ministers had sympathized with the UGC's efforts to cut student numbers (although as much out of a desire to restrain public expenditure as for academic reasons).

But in the mid-1980s the political climate began a decisive shift. Impressive productivity gains had been achieved in the polytechnics apparently without any decline in standards, soothing doubts about both public expenditure and academic quality. At the same time, ministers became aware of the political advantages of wider access. Belatedly, the UGC tacked to the new political wind, abandoning its (never very successful) attempt to persuade universities to cut their intakes. University leaders not only felt that they had been wrong-footed by the polytechnics, now increasingly seen as rivals for political favour, but also that the more generous expansionary intentions of the 1960s had been needlessly abandoned. So at the beginning of the 1990s, rapid expansion resumed in the universities, just when growth rates in some polytechnics began to decline either because of the need to take academic stock or because serious logistical problems were being encountered.

It is possible therefore that the growth differential opened up by the polytechnics in the course of the 1980s will narrow during the 1990s. The establishment of a unified Universities and Colleges Admissions System (UCAS) may reduce the demand for places in the least favoured institutions, if only because candidates are able to make fewer applications in aggregate. The abandonment of the binary system (which, of course, led to the creation of a unified admissions system) may erode the distinctiveness of the former polytechnics. Most of the old universities have learned the assumed lesson of the 1980s, namely that there is safety and success in growth. Donnish objections to over-rapid expansion carry little weight in institutions which have slowly but surely espoused the managerial message of the Jarratt Report (CVCP 1985). In any case, it is possible to exaggerate the numerical advantage gained by the former polytechnics during the 1980s. In 1990 the 34 English universities enrolled 318,000 students while the 30 polytechnics enrolled 319,000 (DfE 1993c). The two sets of institutions were evenly matched (although the universities had more full-time students). It was the 56 colleges of higher education with 116,000 students and local authority colleges with a further 121,000 which tilted the balance against the university sector.

Two further aspects of the growth in student numbers deserve to be mentioned in the context of the university curriculum. The first is that both Scotland with 137,000 students and Wales with 134,000 continue to be over-represented – by 44 per cent and 130 per cent, respectively. As both Scotland and Wales now have separate funding councils, this over-representation is likely to increase. Despite the percentages, the over-representation of Scotland is more significant. Much of the over-representation of Wales is explained by the inflow of English students, not always of the highest calibre if A Level grades are taken as a guide. The Scottish system is much more self-contained. Moreover, Scottish universities not only embody distinctive intellectual values, which are reflected in a distinctive curriculum, but also form the apex of an educational system with different academic practices and social and cultural links. Although it is unlikely that the powerful influence of the Scottish universities over English (and US) higher education in the late eighteenth and early nineteenth centuries will be reproduced 200 years later, the Scottish dimension may become more prominent within the UK system – in the curriculum as well as in matters of funding.

The second aspect of student number growth is that, as a result of specific European Community programmes such as ERASMUS and more generally of the UK's closer engagement in the EC, the number of EC students in UK universities has increased much more rapidly than that of students from other parts of the world. In a single year (1990–1 compared with 1989–90) their number grew five times as fast as that of other overseas students. This growth, of course, is supported by a range of staff exchanges, joint courses and other forms of curricular collaboration. Although the total number of EC students remains small (21,000 in 1990–1), the rapid rate of growth reinforced by these other initiatives makes it likely that the 'Europeanization' of the university curriculum will be a powerful characteristic of the 1990s.

New patterns of funding

The public character of UK higher education remains unchallenged despite the move towards much wider access and consequently greatly increased student numbers. With the exception, that proves the rule, of the University of Buckingham all universities and colleges have continued to be public institutions (although not state institutions on the general European model – a significant distinction). The historic trend away from a semi-private higher education system made up of autonomous and largely self-supporting institutions towards a public system of accountable institutions largely tax-supported has not been reversed, despite the Conservative Government's commitment to wide-scale privatization and the keenness of university leaders to diversify their income base by attracting significant private funds. The expansion of higher education over the past decade has been predominantly financed through 'efficiency gains', the more productive use of available public resources.

Block grants to institutions

Despite complaints about budget cuts, public expenditure on higher education has continued to grow, faster than inflation but not at a sufficient pace to keep up with growing student numbers. At the beginning of the 1980s it came to £1.7 billion – £1,013 million for the universities and £680 million for the polytechnics and colleges. In 1990–91 the total had grown to £2.7 billion – £1,661 million for the universities and £1,014 million for the rest of higher education. The 60:40 split between the allocations to the two sectors remained virtually unchanged over this ten-year period, which suggests that any additional public revenue gained by the polytechnics and colleges was confined to the extra tuition fee income they earned by recruiting more students.

This conclusion, that the polytechnics failed to translate their political success into extra funding during the 1980s, is supported by statistics on the respective 'efficiency gains' in the two sectors. Universities were able to keep unit costs stable in the first half of the 1980s, a back-handed compliment to the UGC's doomed determination to protect the unit of resource. In contrast unit costs in the polytechnics and colleges fell sharply – by more than one-fifth between 1980–1 and 1983–4. In the next half decade they fell by another fifth, while university unit costs declined by only 5 per cent. More recently, impressive 'efficiency gains' have been made in the old university sector because of the sharp rise in student numbers overall and the enthusiasm of some universities for recruiting large numbers of fees-only students. As a result, unit costs in the old universities and former polytechnics have tended to converge again. But in real terms the funding gap is wider in the early 1990s than it was a decade earlier. These funding trends are summarized in Table 1.2.

During the same period, the methods by which funds are allocated to individual institutions have been substantially modified. Up to the end of the 1970s, funds in both sectors had been distributed according to rough-and-ready formulae based on a mixture of historic costs and student head-counts. Although the technical details of the funding systems operated by the UGC, centrally, and local education authorities, centrally through the advanced further education pool and severally at their own discretion, differed, their substance was similar. In 1981 the UGC broke the mould by distributing its much reduced grant on a highly selective basis, although at the time its members imagined they were simply continuing the past practice of so-called 'informed prejudice' under which the best universities – or, rather, departments – were favoured at the expense of the less good, both categories as defined by the university establishment's folk wisdom. However, because under the straitened circumstances of the 1980s selectivity had more extreme effects (both Salford and Aston universities were faced with cuts in their UGC grants of more than 40 per cent over three years), 'informed prejudice' had to be abandoned and replaced by more defensible forms of discrimination. The most notable was the UGC's (later the UFC's) research assessment exercises which attempted to measure the quality of every university department on a four-point scale, ranging from 1 (no research worthy of baseline budget support) to 5 (research of international standing). The third and most recent round of research assessment was extended to the polytechnics and colleges, although on a voluntary basis. In the new unified system more than one-fifth of the total resources allocated to higher education is devoted to the support of 'active researchers', predominantly in accordance with these departmental assessments although allowances are also made for industrial links and development potential. Well over 80 per cent goes to the old universities.

Table 1.2 Funding trends in higher education (1987–94).

Sector	1987–88 (actual)	1988–89 (actual)	1989–90 (actual)	1990–91 (actual)	1991–92 (actual)	1992–93 (provisional)	1993–94 (estimated)
Universities (UK)[1]	100	98	95				
Universities (UK)[1]	100	98	100	93	87	83	
Polytechnics and colleges (England)[2]							
PCFC[1]			100	92	85	81	
HEFCE[3]			100	92	85	80	78

1. The indices for universities and the PCFC are derived from a division of the total UGC/UFC or PCFC recurrent grant and tuition fee income for home and EC students by the financial year average of full-time equivalent student numbers. Figures in the first line for universities include all home and EC fee income. Figures in the second line include fee income from publicly funded students only. All indices were calculated by the Committee of Vice-Chancellors and Principals.

2. The index for polytechnics and colleges is derived from a division of their aggregate expenditure (gross of tuition fees but including miscellaneous income) by financial year full-time equivalent student numbers.

3. Efficiency gains for the HEFCE sector are greater than those of the UFC and PCFC sectors individually; the PCFC institutions, which have lower unit costs when research funding is taken into account, have grown more rapidly and so reduced further the unit cost of higher education as a whole.

Sources: DfE Survey, Further Education Student Record, Universities' Statistical Record

If the research allocation system is largely a development of policies devised for the university sector by the UGC and later the UFC, the system for distributing the much larger allocations for teaching is derived from the practice of the non-university sector. In 1982 the newly established NAB began to develop a funding system that, in the first place, allocated funds more exactly in proportion to (weighted) student numbers and, secondly, to reward those polytechnics and colleges willing to expand. This system was supplemented by targeted and earmarked funds to stimulate research and encourage provision for disadvantaged students. Its principles were further developed by the PCFC after 1988 into a more sophisticated allocation methodology based on institutions bidding competitively for a growing fraction of the available funds, although the NAB's selective initiatives were dropped as too *dirigiste*. (Later the PCFC reversed its hands-off policy by awarding extra funding and places to institutions judged to provide high-quality courses.)

These twin principles, of matching funds to actual student numbers and rewarding growth, were tentatively adopted by the UGC and disastrously developed by its successor, the UFC, which attempted to coerce universities into bidding against each other for all the funds available but sold the game by publishing 'guide prices'. This bid to introduce an 'internal market' into the university sector was frustrated by the universities' unwillingness to play beggar-my-neighbour in the absence of substantial additional resources. By the time the UFC and PCFC were abolished and replaced by a unified higher education funding council, both councils were applying broadly compatible funding systems, allocating funded student places in response to institutional bids embedded in strategic plans.

Tuition fees and student support

Direct allocations to institutions, through the funding councils, represent only part of the income they derive from public expenditure. Another important source is tuition fees paid on behalf of UK students. In 1989, the Conservative Government doubled tuition fees and cut the grants paid to institutions by the UFC and PCFC correspondingly. Its intention was to strengthen the 'market' element in its expenditure on higher education and to weaken the 'planning' element – and, more specifically, to provide institutions with an incentive to recruit extra students. Expenditure on tuition fees had never been cash-limited, because students were entitled to have their fees paid and also to receive grants, and since 1990, loans.

So long as tuition fees remained low, however, institutions had little incentive to take more students than the funded totals allocated to them by the UFC or PCFC. Although universities and polytechnics could always have earned extra income by recruiting off-quota students, few did so on a substantial scale because they had no desire to erode their unit costs over and above the 'efficiency gains' required by the funding councils. Moreover, until 1986 the Government made it clear to both the UGC and the NAB that total public expenditure on higher education (institutional grants plus tuition fees and student grants) was notionally cash-limited. If expenditure on fees was higher than anticipated, grants would be cut correspondingly.

When tuition fees were doubled, institutions for the first time had a real incentive to recruit fees-only students. And, because the UFC and PCFC grant had been cut, they knew that refusal to recruit such students would not protect them from further reductions in unit costs; rather the reverse. The new policy, therefore, produced a significant shift in institutional behaviour. Reluctance to expand without matching funds was abandoned. Controversies about the (declining) 'unit of resource', which had dominated much of higher education policymaking (on both sides of the binary line), subsided. Although the former polytechnics led the way in recruiting large numbers of fees-only students, some universities were not far behind in their enthusiasm. By 1992, 40 per cent of students in one, Keele, were fees-only. Student numbers rose rapidly while unit costs fell. From the Government's perspective this outcome was doubly desirable. Not only was the supply of places increased to match rising demand from school-leavers and adult students, but also significant 'efficiency gains' were made. Instead of being a high-cost low-volume system, UK higher education seemed to be moving rapidly towards becoming a low-cost high-volume system.

More recently, the policy of keeping tuition fees high and institutional grants low to encourage what came to be known as 'efficient expansion' ran into serious difficulties – and, even, into reverse. First, its very success highlighted the serious implications for public expenditure represented by the open-ended commitment to pay tuition fees, and grants/loans, for all the extra students institutions cared to admit. In November 1992, prompted by the Treasury, the Department for Education cut fee levels for students in Arts and Social Science, where most of the fees-only growth had been concentrated, and froze those for other students. Twelve months later fees were cut again, for Arts and Social Science from £1,300 to £750 and from £2,770 to £1,600 for laboratory-based subjects. As a result of this two-stage retreat, the balance between institutional grants and tuition fees was restored to what it had been in 1989. The intention was to reduce the incentive to expand, although it is unclear that this would be the effect if it were left to institutions. Many institutions are so heavily committed to further growth, in both their academic and financial plans, that it is difficult for them to contemplate a slow-down. As a result, the HEFCs have been instructed by the Government to plan on the assumption that there will be a period of consolidation. Funding will be based on 'this assumption about student numbers irrespective of actual enrolments' (DfE 1993d). The Government's primary purpose, of course, is to restrain public expenditure more than to restrain student growth. But so long as students are entitled to have their tuition fees paid, ministers cannot afford to be indifferent to the total number enrolled in universities and colleges despite their attachment to 'market' incentives.

Secondly, the funding councils have failed to find a satisfactory way to take account of fees-only students in determining their own future allocations to institutions. These students cannot be included in funded student place totals easily or quickly. If they were, institutions would be free to recruit fees-only students recklessly, knowing that they would have to bear the burden of lower unit costs only briefly on their own; in later years it would be spread across the system, including those institutions which have expanded more slowly and not earned extra fee income. On the other hand the funding councils cannot ignore the build-up in fees-only students for too long. Otherwise an unacceptably wide gap will open up between the 'system' as represented by funded student places and reality. Sensible planning would be impossible in these circumstances. Although the reduction in fee levels has made this second dilemma less acute for the time being, when expansion resumes in the late 1990s it will re-emerge. The funding councils must also find ways to avoid penalizing expansionary institutions with high proportions of fees-only students, which would be the effect of refusing to recognize that such students exist. To do so would undermine the Government's wider-access policy which has only been temporarily suspended and would discourage fees-only student-led growth in the future. Although the funding councils have bobbed and weaved in their search for technical solutions to these problems created by fees-only students, the underlying difficulty of combining a funding system of top-down block grants to institutions with a bottom-up system of, in effect, student vouchers remains. The speed at which the funding councils will achieve the declared objective of a convergence of 'average units of council funding' remains in question.

The final element in public expenditure on higher education is the total spent on student support. Here three significant trends can be observed. First, because of financial pressure on local education authorities, discretionary awards have all but dried up. Students on courses that do not attract mandatory awards or who are ineligible for such awards now have to support themselves out of their own private resources. Secondly, the value of student grants has declined, forcing many of those students who are fortunate enough to receive mandatory awards to supplement their income by working or parental subsidy. Thirdly, the Government in 1990 introduced a system of student loans. At first the intention was that grants would be frozen at their existing cash levels and loans increased until they are equal in value. But in November 1993 grants were actually cut to speed up the switch from grants to loans. To soften the blow the Government has introduced modest 'access funds' for distribution by institutions to deserving students (although official guidance implies that those students who refuse to take out loans are not eligible).

Some of the implications for the university curriculum of these new patterns of funding are obvious. The inadequacy of student support means that many students are no longer able to devote all their time and energy to their courses, although Britain's short three- and four-year degrees demand intensive and concentrated commitment from students. Others are less clear.

The recruitment of fees-only students may encourage institutions to regard these students as voucher-holders who must be wooed, especially in less popular subjects. Yet many institutions clearly regard them as marginal-cost 'making-up-the-numbers' students. The relentless 'efficiency gains' of the past decade have had a direct impact on the curriculum. Class sizes have increased and course options have been reduced. However, there are signs that some teachers and managers have begun to appreciate that a mass system – necessarily lower if not low-cost and desirably high-volume – cannot afford, academically as well as financially, simply to offer a debased version of an élite curriculum. A more positive outlook needs to be developed. The university curriculum must be more purposefully managed if students, by being offered inappropriate courses and unimaginative teaching, are not to be robbed of the benefits of wider access.

References

Birch, W. (1988) *The Challenge to Higher Education*. Society for Research into Higher Education/Open University Press, Milton Keynes.

Committee of Vice-Chancellors and Principals (1985) *Report of the Steering Group for Efficiency Studies in Universities* (Jarratt Report). CVCP, London.

Department for Education (1992) *Education Statistics for the United Kingdom 1992*. HMSO, London.

Department for Education (1993a) *Education Statistics for the United Kingdom – 1993 edition* (Statistical Bulletin 2/93). DfE, London.

Department for Education (1993b) *GCSE and A/AS Examination Results 1991/92* (Statistical Bulletin 15/93). DfE, London.

Department for Education (1993c) *Student Numbers in Higher Education – Great Britain 1980/81 to 1990/91* (Statistical Bulletin 17/93). DfE, London.

Department for Education (1993d) Letter from Roger Dawe, Deputy Secretary, to Graeme Davies, Chief Executive of the HEFCE, 12 November.

Robinson, E. (1968) *The New Polytechnics: A Radical Policy for Higher Education*. Cornmarket Press, London.

Scott, P. (1993) in *The Transition from Élite to Mass Higher Education* (Occasional Paper Series). Higher Education Division, Department of Employment, Education and Training, Canberra.

Trow, M. (1973) *Problems in the Transition from Élite to Mass Higher Education*. Carnegie Commission on Higher Education, Berkeley.

2

Managing the Curriculum: Roles and Responsibilities

Peter Scott and David Watson

The title of this chapter asserts that the higher education curriculum must be managed more explicitly and actively than has been customary in the past, and argues more broadly for a closer association between the management of universities and colleges and the organization of teaching and learning within them. These are a controversial assertion and argument. The management of the curriculum, if this is taken to mean that decisions about its aims and objectives, content, teaching methods and patterns of assessment are taken by others than those intimately engaged in its delivery, is seen by many teachers in higher education, especially in the traditional universities, potentially as a threat to academic freedom, an invasion of student–teacher intimacy, a denial of professional expertise and an assault on collegiality (Scott 1994). Indeed, the very notion of the 'curriculum' is regarded by some as unduly reductionist and restrictive, incompatible with the open-ended character of the academic enterprise.

Such criticisms are certainly exaggerated. Nevertheless, they are widespread. The fears that lie behind them must be taken seriously: for managerial reasons because higher education is a people-intensive industry, and the success of institutions depends heavily on the commitment (and so the morale) of their staffs; and for intellectual reasons because the management of knowledge, its primary resource in teaching as in research, cannot by its very nature be centralized (Popper 1961). The argument in this chapter, therefore, is twofold: first, that a closer association between institutional management and the curriculum is inevitable and, secondly, that contrary to these fears this association has clear academic benefits.

The first part of this argument is straightforward. When most courses were single-subject honours degrees provided by autonomous universities comprising an élite system of higher education over which the so-called academic guild had a predominant influence, it might have been possible to regard the curriculum as a private matter, at the near-total discretion of teachers either organized in faculties and departments or individually. In this academic Arcadia 'managers' had yet to be invented. Instead, administrators or 'support staff' (the language was revealing) serviced the guild.

This Arcadia has long since vanished, if it ever existed. Even in élite universities the guild always had to share ownership of the curriculum with professional bodies in subjects like Medicine and Engineering, although in the former leaders of the guild and profession were often the same and always similar people. In the former polytechnics and the colleges of higher education, of course, teachers were never free to determine the curriculum on their own. Courses had to be approved by a range of outside agencies ranging from the Council for National Academic Awards and other validating bodies, on which teachers were well represented, to administrative organizations like regional advisory councils and the Department of Education and Science. Moreover, the delivery of these courses was subject to external scrutiny by HM Inspectors. Initial Teacher Education has been particularly under central direction in curriculum terms as well as the planning of numbers, and the new Teacher Training Agency for England will confirm this (DfE 1993).

More recently, further changes have reduced the autonomy of the curriculum. The most dramatic is the rapid expansion in student numbers. Here change has been qualitative as well as quantitative. Institutions, which formerly were collegial and hierarchical, have been transformed into large and complex organizations by the sheer scale of expansion, while new kinds of students, who neither possess an 'academic culture' as part of their family tradition nor aspire to join the élite professions, form an increasingly significant fraction of the total student population. As a result, more active management practices have had to be adopted in place of the passive administrative culture which once prevailed in much of higher education, especially in the traditional universities. In particular, institutional managers have been forced to become most active in two sensitive arenas: improving productivity because budget increases have not matched the rise in student numbers; and maintaining the quality of courses despite these productivity gains (as well as providing public reassurance). Both lead them into the heart of the curriculum.

Many courses are now offered in subjects defined in terms of their vocational relevance rather than their academic coherence, most notably perhaps in Business and other applied social and economic studies and in Technology. In these new fields, as well as in professional courses more precisely and traditionally defined, teachers must give greater weight to the views of active practitioners in designing an appropriate curriculum. The structure of courses has also been radically modified. The growing popularity of modular degree schemes and of credit accumulation and transfer systems means that students, as customers, have begun to play a more active role in shaping their courses.

New patterns of course assessment, which now place more emphasis on negotiated projects and less on terminal examinations, both reflect and reinforce a more equal balance of responsibilities between teachers and learners. New teaching technologies have radically changed the conditions, intellectual as well as logistical, under which the curriculum is delivered and have disrupted traditional patterns of pedagogy. A new cadre of para-academics has developed alongside mainstream teachers: counsellors to guide students through the modular and credit maze, software engineers, graphic designers and other 'systems' people to design programs for the new technologies, as well as librarians and other more conventional 'support' staff. Severally and together with teachers they have become 'curriculum managers'. The cumulative effect of all these changes has been to transform the management of the curriculum from an inner-directed and artisanal process into an outer-directed and quasi-industrial operation. Once a 'secret garden' of donnish prescription, the curriculum must now be managed.

The second part of the argument, that these changes can lead to academic gains, is less straightforward. Professional status and academic freedom appear to have been eroded while managerial power has been enhanced. However, a more balanced assessment is possible. If teachers are reluctant to accept that the university curriculum must be explicitly managed, a mismatch between professional values, myths even, and curricular practice is likely to grow, with a number of baleful consequences. Their interests will suffer, but so too will those of institutional managers. First, many of the reforms needed to open up higher education to a wider student constituency will be seen, perhaps wrongly, as managerially (and externally) imposed rather than academically (and internally) generated. As a result they may be regarded primarily as labour-control measures and embraced only with reluctance or rancour. Encouraging sullen professional opposition, even unwittingly, is hardly in the interests of institutional managers. It will make their job more difficult and render their efforts less effective. The pace of reform may be slowed and its intentions frustrated. Both equal opportunities, or the fairer distribution of democratic life-chances, and economic efficiency, if higher education is truly the engine of post-industrial productivity, will be undermined.

Secondly, these reforms are likely to be implemented in a myopic and Philistine fashion if largely shaped by managers divorced from the enthusiasms and pressures of university and college teaching and ignorant of, or indifferent to, the closely woven contextuality of the disciplines around which institutional sub-structures and professional identities are still organized. Awkwardly and ineptly imposed reforms which lack adequate philosophical or cultural grounding are hardly in the best interests of teachers. Grandiose rhetoric which calls as witnesses Newman or Humboldt may encourage a misleading account of the origins and imperatives of the modern university (Scott 1993). Nevertheless current reforms must be related to the university's historic purposes. They have not sprung out of an instantaneous and featureless present. But, if teachers adopt negative or passive attitudes to the reform of higher education, at the heart of which is the management of the curriculum, academic values will play only a secondary role in determining its purposes and priorities. Adversarial attitudes will flourish with the new para-academic cadre siding with the managers against the teachers rather than supporting both.

Thirdly, the intellectual creativity likely to be released by the opening up of higher education, and consequent redefinition of inherited scholarly standards and vocational categories, will go unrealized if teachers are not willing and active partners in the enterprise. The quality of both student learning and, more broadly of intellectual life, could be impoverished. It is important to remember that the traditions, whether expressed through a general intellectual culture or through the academic values of individual disciplines, which appear to be threatened by today's managerial reforms, are themselves the expression of earlier encounters between the university and society. Universities played an important role first in promoting the urban culture of the age of the Industrial Revolution and later, when the city provided too narrow a stage, in providing an alternative institutional form (Bender 1993). The formation of professions, and so elaboration of professional education, are direct consequences of the growth of a 'professional society' in late nineteenth and twentieth century Britain (Perkin 1989). The modern university was decisively shaped by the imperatives of war-time mobilization and peace-time social reform and economic investment.

The themes of current reforms, some benign like the opening up of higher education, others more contested such as the efforts to create more responsive higher education institutions able to meet the needs of their student customers and to play a leading role within a wider 'knowledge industry', are themselves a reflection of the socio-economic order of the late twentieth century. They too are likely to produce exciting intellectual reverberations and contribute to cultural shifts, which will form the 'traditions' of the twenty-first century university. The management of the curriculum is the reform most directly implicated in this revision of the university's historic mission and consequently in the restructuring of intellectual life.

This chapter will examine, first, the consequences of the growth of post-binary systems for the size and character of institutions of higher education and, secondly, the implications of the latter for the shape of the university curriculum. This does not mean that the latter is wholly determined by the former. The curriculum is shaped by a variety of more powerful primary forces – the intellectual dynamics of individual subjects, shifting student constituencies, new labour-market demands, changed social and cultural expectations. But these forces are mediated through institutions; hence the concentration here on institutional forms. Institutions are both managerial and normative. They employ teachers, organize courses and offer other learning opportunities, enrol students, credentialize graduates and diplomates. But they also provide an environment within which academic and professional values are realized. In both senses they shape the university curriculum.

The institutional environment

The scale of institutions

Two closely linked phenomena, expansion and massification, characterize the development of modern higher education systems. The first has led to the creation of much larger institutions. The last great wave of expansion in the 1950s and 1960s started from a much lower base in terms of student numbers (and total cost) and occurred at a time when in most Western societies post-war economic growth and a widespread commitment to social planning had produced both the resources and political will necessary to fund this growth out of taxation. This comparative lack of constraint and enthusiasm for grand, publicly sponsored infrastructure projects meant that in the UK and most other European countries, Canada, Australia and the USA many brand-new universities and colleges were founded. The high political visibility (and credit) of institution building more than compensated for the potentially higher costs incurred by this policy. In the second, present, wave of expansion during the 1980s and 1990s changed economic and political conditions have led to demands for cost-effective growth. In most cases this has meant expanding existing institutions, which is likely to yield significant efficiency gains, rather than establishing new ones, which require expensive up-front investment in infrastructure.

As a result of the expansion of student numbers, the average size of universities is rising rapidly, a significant shift because UK universities until now have been small by international standards. Arguably their ethos, which decisively shapes the university curriculum, is a function of their scale. The University of London, an exceptional institution and perhaps on the brink of dissolution, is only a third of the size of the University of California, which is typical of large US state universities despite its global eminence. These larger institutions may be produced by merging old and new universities to form comprehensive multi-campus universities of sufficient size to reconcile the apparently contradictory goals of wider access and research excellence.

In the short term, at any rate, the logistical difficulties of creating comprehensive universities, and the managerial energy such efforts would absorb, are likely to outweigh any benefits of economies of scale or larger academic critical mass. The former polytechnics are also almost certain to wish to establish their new credentials as universities before contemplating mergers in which their separate identities would be dissolved. However, mergers involving smaller colleges of higher education are more likely. Denied the title 'university colleges', they appear to have only a marginal role to play in the new post-binary system. Some colleges will identify appropriate niches but others may cut and run into the embrace of neighbouring universities. However, any university–college mergers will be a secondary factor in producing much larger institutions. The primary factor will be the growth of student numbers described earlier in this chapter that is unlikely to be seriously checked by the Government's decision to reduce the incentive to recruit fees-only students by reducing or freezing tuition fee levels.

Not all universities will grow at the same rate. Many campus universities established in the 1960s are unlikely to be able to grow substantially, despite the ambitious targets of their founders, because of the lack of sufficient capital funds for new buildings and the lack of a supporting urban infrastructure. They will be constrained by their green-fields origins. The expansion of the technological universities may also be restricted because of their subject balance. Engineering and other applied sciences are expensive to teach and have experienced recruitment difficulties. Consequently these universities will find over-rapid growth, leading inexorably to greater-than-average productivity gains, an unattractive option. In any case, student demand is less buoyant than in the Arts and Social Sciences.

Instead, growth will probably be concentrated in the civic and red-brick universities in the former UFC sector and the urban new universities in the former PCFC sector, although shortages of suitable accommodation may restrict expansion in the latter. Already among the largest institutions, many are in large metropolitan centres, which makes accommodation for full-time students less of a constraint and enhances their capacity to recruit part-time and non-standard students, and offer a comprehensive range of subjects, so maximizing their growth potential across disciplines. Just as the 'new' universities of the 1960s were the emblematic institutions of the Robbins expansion, these big urban universities, once in the nineteenth and early twentieth centuries agents of an earlier expansion, may become the emblematic institutions of post-binary growth.

Increasing heterogeneity

The second phenomenon characterizing development of modern higher education systems, massification, has led to institutions which are not only much larger but more highly differentiated, internally as well as externally, and so more complex to organize and manage. Universities and, to a lesser extent, colleges of higher education have taken on multiple missions. Sometimes their 'core' businesses have become more difficult to define. Although student growth has been an important factor, it is not the only or necessarily the most important one. Even if there had been no growth, universities would still have had to cope with increasing heterogeneity. Even those (few) universities which have expanded only modestly over the past decades have been affected.

One cause of this heterogeneity is the growing turbulence of the 'private world' of knowledge, skills and disciplines. New subjects, often with a pronounced vocational orientation, have been added to the university curriculum. Often they have been more difficult to absorb than older professional subjects like Law, Medicine or Engineering – partly because the vocations to which they relate do not enjoy such a high status and partly because, in some cases, their ethos is critical, even subversive, of traditional academic values. But intellectual heterogeneity is also characteristic of established disciplines. Some have become fiercely reductionist, loyal to a rigid scientism; others have embraced with fervour eclecticism and even relativism. As a result of the growth of new subjects and shifts within old ones, the incommensurability of individual disciplines has increased. The sharing of academic values, which precede and support institutional loyalties, has become more difficult.

A more significant cause of heterogeneity, however, is to be found in the radical changes in the 'public world' of universities and colleges, some of which have been described in the preceding section of this chapter. Three particular aspects deserve further discussion in this context – the diversity of new (and old) student populations, mixed messages from the labour market, and the growth of a more differentiated post-binary pattern of higher education.

Although students have become powerful stakeholders in higher education, their growing influence in shaping the character of institutions is likely to have an uneven, and unpredictable, effect on the character of institutions and so the shape of the curriculum. But heterogeneity is the key. In one sense they may become less discriminating consumers. The mass recruitment of school-leavers is sucking into the system many students who lack a clear academic commitment or coherent vocational ambitions. Those without 'standard' entry qualifications – A Levels, or Scottish Higher grades – now make up one-third of new entrants, and these students may also lack disciplined study habits and a sharp subject focus (DfE 1992). At the same time, the demarcation between secondary education (knowledge-gathering and skill-acquiring) and higher education (initiation into an intellectual or professional culture) is becoming fuzzier. Universities already recruit many students closer in outlook (and academic standard?) to secondary-school pupils than undergraduates of the recent, although not the more distant, past. In academic terms, universities were at their most élitist between 1945 and 1980, after the scholarship boys (and girls) had begun to displace the gentleman-undergraduate and before mass expansion had got under way.

In the USA the feel of many higher education institutions is similar to that of the high school. The same transformation of ethos may take place as the UK moves towards mass higher education. The impact on the university curriculum will be profound. The danger, of course, is that universities will attempt to maintain an academic 'gold standard' and regard the catching-up strategies they have to adopt for a growing number of students as remedial and exceptional, deviations from an inflexible norm, rather than seeking to renegotiate the boundaries between secondary, further and higher education.

On the other hand, a mass higher education system recruits a growing number of new kinds of student, part-timers, those admitted under special 'Access' programmes or without standard entry qualifications and mature students. Many bring to their studies a rich experience of life and work, which can be used to transform the curriculum at its heart. But again there is a danger their presence will be seen as an administrative headache rather than an intellectual challenge. The impact of part-time, 'Access' and mature students goes far beyond devising user-friendly course structures and allowing credit for prior or experiential learning. Their growing prominence in higher education will transform traditional relationships between teachers and students. The university curriculum is no longer largely owned by the former; instead it becomes a joint enterprise. Universities and colleges, therefore, have to cope both with far less sophisticated students and with students who possess knowledge and skills different from but equal to those of their teachers, as well as a strong sense of 'entitlement' derived from the substantial personal investment they have made in order to 'return to study'. No longer is it possible to regard most students as broadly alike. So a uniform curriculum, marginally modified to accommodate 'remedial' or 'non-standard' students, is no longer adequate.

All students, even the best and the brightest recruited by élite institutions, now bring different skills and values to higher education. They have grown up in a visual rather than literary world, dominated by the TV sound-byte or the instantaneous tyranny of 'style' rather than the memorized poem or the long-haul of a cumulative high culture. The shift from inner-direction to outer-direction identified by David Riesman in mid-twentieth century America, intensified by the commodification of youth culture, has produced a transformed world (Riesman 1950). These radical effects have been reflected in changes in primary and secondary schools often inadequately interpreted as a loss of rigour and decline in standards. In one sense the globalization of social trends and cultural habits has produced a homogeneity of response and so cannot logically be identified as a cause of heterogeneity within higher education. But in two other senses such identification remains plausible. First, this apparent homogeneity has coalesced around non-cognitive values and practices which may be hostile to those institutionalized in the university. Secondly, this homogeneity masks profound differences; the agreement is to disagree.

Shifts in the labour market are also likely to encourage heterogeneity. Despite the proliferation of university–industry links over the past decade, it can be argued that the articulation between a mass higher education system and the labour market is weaker than when a narrower system of universities and colleges had a sharper vocational focus. The alignment of élite institutions, élite students and élite jobs is far more exact than it can be in a sprawling post-secondary system the primary role of which is mass socialization. In some parts, of course, post-experience vocational education for example, the link to jobs is direct, but in others (like the modular undergraduate degree schemes taken by large numbers of students) it is at best oblique.

It is not only higher education which is changing; the labour market is becoming increasingly volatile under post-industrial conditions. Its messages are more difficult to interpret because the growth of flexible employment is undermining the notion of long-haul linear careers and because the pattern of industry is being radically (and continuously) reshaped by technology. There is an alarming oscillation between a demand for ever more expert 'knowledge' and highly synoptic 'skills'. On the one hand the development of a 'knowledge society' in which the production of this knowledge and skills has become a central economic function seems to make higher education a key component of wealth generation rather than, as in the past, a servicing agency which provides raw material in the shape of science, technology and trained graduates. On the other hand, in such a society only a small proportion of graduates is likely to join that élite cadre of symbolic experts; many more will be deskilled (Drucker 1993).

The differentiation, internal and external, of institutions has also been encouraged by the movement towards a post-binary arrangement of higher education. The abandonment of the binary system in the UK is only one example of a wider international trend towards post-binaryism. A unified system of higher education was established in Sweden in 1977 embracing the smaller regional university colleges as well as the 11 traditional universities. At the same time teacher training, nursing and other specialized colleges were incorporated in larger universities or university colleges (Scott 1991). Ten years later, the binary division in Australia, into universities and colleges of advanced education, was abandoned (Moses 1993). The creation of a unified system in England has raised hopes in the rest of Europe that non-university institutions there can follow the example of the former polytechnics, especially on the part of higher professional schools in the Netherlands but even in the German *Fachhochschulen*.

The move towards post-binary systems, however, has not led to greater uniformity among hitherto different types of institutions. Instead rough-cut differentiation of roles between sectors has been replaced by fine-grain differentiation of function between and within individual institutions. Institutions must now take responsibility for determining their own missions, and putting them into operational effect through strategic and business plans, rather than being allocated broad sectoral identities. Smaller universities and colleges, of course, may seek to maintain their homogeneity by searching out niches in the marketplace of mass higher education. But larger universities have little choice but to embrace heterogeneity. In a post-binary system they must adopt more comprehensive roles, even if their former missions as UFC or PCFC institutions offer a broad guide at first. This pattern of convergence (between sectors), divergence (among institutions) and differentiation (within institutions) is much too complex a phenomenon to be characterized, or stigmatized, as 'academic drift'.

Several 'old' universities with strong research records, large numbers of research and other postgraduate students and high-quality undergraduate applicants nevertheless are actively developing wider-access policies, by sponsoring special 'Access' courses or negotiating franchising partnerships with further education colleges. Also Government and funding council policies are leading to greater internal differentiation. Separate funding streams for teaching and research have begun to produce a more marked division of labour between departments and among individuals. Three rounds of research assessment have led to departments with international reputations co-existing in the same institution with departments with a dwindling commitment to research. Quality assessment, of courses and teaching, is likely to produce similar differentiation.

Institutional management

These much larger and more heterogeneous universities have to be managed in new ways. Institutions with up to about 5,000 full-time-equivalent (FTE) students, or 7,000 if their students are mainly full-time and their missions uncomplicated, can perhaps be managed along collegial lines – in other words, academic self-government assisted by a professional (but largely passive) administration. However, collegial management, in its familiar and regretted form, may only be appropriate for institutions with a high degree of autonomy in an élite higher education system. Therefore it may have become a historic form rather than a current option.

Institutions with between 7,000 and about 15,000 FTEs need to be managed on different terms. A cadre of senior managers drawn from both academic and administrative staffs, assisted by professional managers in areas like finance and personnel, is created. In this new corporate culture 'executive' replaces 'administrative' as the dominant ethos. The strategic direction of institutions can no longer afford to be set in negotiations among academics who then leave their decisions to be implemented by administrators. Not only is there a lack of common ground among academics, for the reasons discussed earlier, but the implementation of often incommensurable objectives by a heterogeneous institution within a complex environment demands high-grade managerial skills. It is this transition from 'collegial' to 'managerial' cultures which many UK institutions have experienced in the past decade. Although different in political conception, the drive for greater efficiency in universities begun by the 1985 Jarratt Report and the incorporation of the polytechnics and colleges following the Education Reform Act 1988 can plausibly be regarded as aspects of the same drive towards managerialism.

It can be argued, however, that institutions with significantly more than 15,000 FTE students, a threshold that many British universities will approach and several will pass in the next five years, are best managed in a third way which some have described as 'post-Fordist'. Radical differentiation within institutions compromises the case for strong centralized direction which had been strengthened by the earlier move towards greater heterogeneity. The senior management, the locus of most decision-making in the earlier 'managerial' phase, shrinks to a slimmed-down strategic core.

Its job is to safeguard the financial (and legal) integrity and the academic mission of the university, and to provide management services to its basic units which enjoy an operational freedom that goes far beyond responsibility for devolved budgets. As a result institutional hierarchies become much flatter, or are replaced by loosely-coupled networks. This pattern is typical of how many successful private corporations are now managed, particularly and significantly those in knowledge-intensive industries which employ highly-skilled workers.

This transition from 'managerial' to 'strategic' cultures may appear to give back to faculties, departments, units and even individuals the power they lost during the earlier move from 'collegial' to 'managerial' cultures. While such an outcome would be welcome in many universities, it might be misinterpreted outside the university, especially by politicians as a retreat from the hard-nosed managerialism which had successfully steered higher education through the turbulence of the past decade during which such impressive gains had been made in both productivity and accountability. In fact, neither perception would be accurate. The move towards a 'strategic' management culture in universities is neither a retreat to old-style collegiality, a vain attempt to re-create a lost donnish dominion, nor a retreat from managerialism but a reinterpretation and recombination of both to meet the radically different challenge of managing mass institutions.

A changing university curriculum

The new environment in which universities and colleges must operate and the consequent changes in institutional size, character and management have had a fundamental impact on the ethos of higher education and so potentially on the nature of the university curriculum. The exceptionalism of UK higher education, certainly compared with mass institutions in the USA (although not prestigious private universities and liberal-arts colleges) and most universities in continental Europe, and the peculiar intimacy characteristic of its undergraduate education depend to a large degree on institutional arrangements which may already be anachronistic. The UK system is no longer exceptional, certainly in terms of access. Its curricular intimacy too may be difficult to sustain in much larger and heterogeneous institutions. But that exceptionalism and intimacy reflect a knot of values which remain influential in measuring quality, defining excellence and determining success. Paradoxically in their drive to make universities, and departments within them, more accountable, managers, both system-wide and institutional, rely on criteria derived from an academic value-system which they are widely seen as undermining.

This tradition of academic and pastoral intimacy, therefore, continues to be relevant within a mass system, although it is on the defensive. It cannot fairly be regarded as an anachronism, the fading echo of a redundant age of élite higher education. Potentially, it offers a creative environment which, at its best, fosters student learning rather than rote teaching. Its academic effectiveness therefore is difficult to question. A case can even be made that this belief in intimacy encourages greater efficiency in more straightforward resource terms. By emphasizing the quality of learning rather than the amount of teaching, it may even justify a reduction in class-contact hours. Its relevance to a customer-led rather than producer-dominated model of higher education can also be argued. The idea of intimacy provides a flexible context in which, for example, learning contracts can be negotiated or prior learning recognized. It is not even incompatible with effective institutional management because, as has already been argued, networks will be more important than hierarchies in the large and heterogeneous universities of the future.

Nor is this commitment to academic intimacy characteristic of only a small part of higher education. Although most intensely realized in the Oxbridge tutorial system, its value was endorsed by the other universities and, by means of the former Council for National Academic Awards, crossed the old binary divide into the former polytechnics and the colleges of higher education. The notion of intimacy, that students and teachers are bound together in a privileged – and, in some sense, private – relationship, was (and is?) a pervasive ideal. In the old universities it has been centred around research, not so much because courses are necessarily constrained (or invigorated) by an active research agenda but because, like research, the best undergraduate curriculum has to be open-ended, flexible, provisional. In the former polytechnics it has been most powerfully expressed through the idea of the primacy of the course, which creates a space in which academic values have priority over administrative practice, territory controlled by lecturers rather than managers. In both cases the links to professional esteem and expertise and to academic freedom are clear.

For these reasons it is probably wrong to draw too sharp a contrast between two models of the university curriculum – one intimate, or internalized, characteristic of élite higher education, and of élite institutions within mass systems; the other formal, or externalized, more suitable for such mass systems. Certainly it is misleading to conclude that, as UK higher education moves to much wider access and universities become much larger and more heterogeneous institutions, the former model will be inexorably displaced by the latter. The alignment of values, and practices, is far from exact. Nevertheless, two processes are at work which are powerfully reshaping the university curriculum.

The first process is a redefinition of both inputs and outputs. In terms of inputs the growth of alternative 'Access' pathways, now being generalized in the context of more pervasive links between further and higher education, and the development of National Vocational Qualifications (NVQs) are both examples of this redefinition. In terms of outputs the drift towards criteria-referenced competences, increasingly expressed through student portfolios and transcripts, and away from the norm-referenced measures of attainment characteristic of traditional honours-degree classifications, is perhaps the most dramatic evidence of redefinition. Of course there is a danger that such redefinition of inputs and outputs will be over-interpreted. 'Access' courses, although perhaps not NVQs, do not challenge conventional assumptions about academic fitness; they merely interpret them more liberally. Also honours degrees are not criteria-free; their criteria are merely internalized rather than explicit.

The second process is the opening up of course structures, in particular the better articulation of student choice and progression. Obvious examples are the development of modular degree schemes, and now the modularization of all courses, undergraduate and postgraduate, across entire institutions, and the growing popularity of credit accumulation and transfer systems (CATS) which generally accompany such developments (Robertson 1994). Not only does initiation of these reforms often depend on managerial initiative at the centre (of the institution or even the system), but successful implementation requires sustained interaction between faculties and departments. In some cases the two processes are elided. A good example is the franchising of courses to further education colleges. A typical pattern is for a dedicated 'Access' course to be redefined as year nought of a degree, largely to make students eligible for grants. The next step is often to franchise the next year, year one of a degree, and later years.

Although this second process, the opening up of the university curriculum, can be regarded as an administrative reorganization rather than an academic reconfiguration of traditional courses, it has radical effects. First, the administrative complexity of such reforms leads to the development of a substantial bureaucracy, opening the door to sustained managerial intervention in the university curriculum. Secondly, new methods for allocating resources within and between institutions become feasible because modularization and CATS provide the essential data for the development of a credit-based funding system. Thirdly, conventional demarcations are weakened, for example between full- and part-time students and, crucially, between completers and non-completers (so eroding the key distinction between success and failure). Finally, the intellectual reverberations of opening-up the university curriculum become too loud to be ignored. Fundamental questions about the aims and intentions of courses must be addressed. In turn, these provoke even more basic questions concerning intellectual taxonomy, which can no longer be informally renegotiated within the profession(s) but can now only be resolved in open and explicit debate.

What is not yet clear is whether these two processes, the redefinition of inputs and outputs and the opening up and articulation of the university curriculum, are incompatible in the long term with the peculiar intimacy characteristic of UK higher education. If the answer is yes, it is unlikely that the traditional pattern of undergraduate education organized round the idea of an honours degree, however modernized and liberalized, can survive. The curriculum will need to be organized instead according to novel and radical principles. Some, enthusiasts for root-and-branch CATS and competences, welcome such a prospect. But if the answer is no, the basic pattern can perhaps be preserved, not necessarily in terms of its detailed organization but of its value-system. These two rival accounts also suggest quite different approaches to managing the university curriculum. The first suggests, indeed requires, a clear break with past practice. The university curriculum must be managed like all other aspects of its operation – and on similar terms. The second implies a more subtle and traditional differentiation. The role of management is to support the curriculum; their relationship is one of means to ends.

New roles and responsibilities

In the past decade higher education institutions, especially perhaps the old universities, have often been criticized for failing to manage change successfully. They stood accused of infirmity of purpose and sclerosis of function. At the same time within higher education a dangerous fissure opened up between academics and managers, contributing to the alienation of the former and feeding the ambition of the latter. Most people expect these twin tensions to increase as the system expands rapidly towards wider access and the pattern of institutions becomes more problematical under postbinary conditions. The managerial shortcomings of many institutions will be more cruelly exposed and academic collegiality further eroded.

It is possible, however, that post-binary expansion may have the opposite effect. The shift to 'strategic' management in the growing number of mass institutions may produce an environment that is both more efficient, in terms of strategic direction and the effective deployment of resources, and more acceptable to the academic community, because it is less threatening to their values than the top-down managerial patterns of government that presently prevail, and because it is more flexible in the face of rapidly changing knowledge and skills. Careful redefinition of the roles of 'managers', 'teachers' and other 'learning support' staff is necessary if educational values are to be preserved and conflict reduced.

The prospects for the university curriculum remain problematic – whether approached from the management of institutions, the intimacy and integrity of teaching, or the multivalent influence of stakeholders. One response is to deplore the apparent collapse of coherence. Another, more hopeful, is to emphasize the opportunities created by this volatility. The trends we have identified can, and should, be responded to positively. A great deal of emphasis has been placed on the political, structural, organizational and managerial aspects of building a post-binary system with wider, if not mass, access. Far too little attention has been paid to the development and delivery of the curriculum within such a system, and to the creative adjustments to be made, by 'managers' as well as 'teachers'. Some of these difficulties, and opportunities, are addressed below, especially in Part 4.

References

Bender, T. (1993) The culture of intellectual life: the city and the professions, in *Intellect and Public Life*. Johns Hopkins University Press, Baltimore.

Department for Education (1992) *Students in Higher Education – England* (Statistical Bulletin 19/92). DfE, London.

Department for Education (1993) *The Government's Proposals for the Reform of Initial Teacher Training*. DfE, London.

Drucker, P. (1993) *Post-Capitalist Society*. Harper Business Books, New York.

Moses, I. (1993) Against the stream: Australia's policy of tertiary integration, in Gellert, C. (ed.) *Higher Education in Europe*. Jessica Kingsley, London.

Perkin, H. (1989) *The Rise of Professional Society: England since 1880*. Routledge, London.

Popper, K. (1961) *The Poverty of Historicism*. Routledge and Kegan Paul, London.

Riesman, D. (1950) *The Lonely Crowd: a study in the changing American character*. Yale University Press, New Haven.

Robertson, D. (1994) *Report of the National CATS Development Project*. Higher Education Quality Council, London.

Scott, P. (1991) *Higher Education in Sweden: a look from the outside*. National Board for Universities and Colleges, Stockholm.

Scott, P. (1993) The idea of the university in the 21st century: a British perspective. *British Journal of Educational Studies*, 41, 1 March.

Scott, P. (1994) *The Impact of CATS on Academic Values and Institutional Loyalties* (Occasional Paper Series). Centre for Policy Studies in Education, University of Leeds.

3

Changing the Subject:
The Organization of Knowledge
and Academic Culture

Robin Middlehurst and Ronald Barnett

Introduction

For several centuries, the heart of academic life has revolved around disciplines or subject areas. These intellectual territories have had powerful and wide-ranging effects, both within the university and beyond it in public and private life. The disciplines have shaped the idea of a university, have provided a means of structuring knowledge and understanding, and have offered a way of organizing access to knowledge and understanding. They have also contributed to the moulding of personal, professional and social identities. The disciplines have evolved and developed over time, along with the universities and their host societies, in a complex flow of give and take as disciplinary shifts have fed and responded to external changes. Consequently (and as Foucault and Bourdieu have indicated), the disciplines have also contributed sites of symbolic power both in the academic world and in the wider society (Bourdieu and Passeron 1979; Rabinow 1984).

At the end of the twentieth century, this image of evolution and accommodation in the relationship between disciplines, universities and society no longer seems appropriate. A number of forces are converging which are causing potentially more fundamental changes in the academic heartland of the disciplines and subject areas. It is our purpose in this chapter to explore the causes of change in these relationships, to examine the nature of changes as they affect 'the subject', and to consider the impact of present changes on academic life, at both managerial and individual levels. We will also speculate as to where these changes might be leading and how they might be dealt with.

Causes of change in higher education

As Scott and Watson have shown in Chapters 1 and 2, the changes which are taking place within UK universities are of several kinds: structural, managerial and cultural. They are also occurring at a rapid rate, if one compares the changes made in the last 15 years, for example, to those occurring in the previous 50 years. A similar rate of change is also affecting life outside the universities as a new phase of post-industrial society is entered (Peters 1989; Beckhard and Pritchard 1992; Makridakis 1992). The variety, the rapidity and the simultaneity of the changes combine to create a perception within universities – a perception which may also be real – that current changes are far-reaching and fundamental. A further perception is that the causes of change are largely external, a perception which has important consequences, yet may not be the entire story.

The four broad trends highlighted by Scott and Watson as creating the conditions in which the curriculum should be more clearly managed – the ending of the binary line, expansion of student numbers, new funding arrangements for higher education and new patterns of student support – already indicate some of the direct causes of change in universities. These can be categorized loosely as legislative, political and financial, and they are all interrelated. However, deeper and more fundamental pressures can also be detected. Two important areas will be picked out, each of which can be tracked into the academic heartland of subjects and disciplines. The interesting point in relation to the internal–external tension outlined above is that the original source of these deeper shifts probably lies in that very heartland which is now coping with the consequences of changes; the causes and consequences have gone full-circle round a loop leading from the disciplines and now back into the disciplines. The image of change that emerges from this depiction is cyclical and interactive rather than linear and reactive, depending on stimuli and responses from both internal and external sources.

Higher education and economic competitiveness

The first pressure that comes into view is overtly economic, but carries social, geographical and cultural undertones. Global economic shifts in the post-war era are increasing the wealth and competitiveness of the Pacific Rim at the expense of many Western economies including the UK (Sparrow 1993). The struggle to keep pace with competitors (old and new) and the consequences of a relative decline in competitiveness, raise questions about the ways in which economic vitality is achieved and sustained. Because of the very different cultural and social traditions of the emerging economies, the causes of their success are sought not only in their different commercial and management practices, but also in their educational and cultural traditions

(Wiener 1985). Whilst observing and learning from the practices of others, a mirror is also being held up to our own educational (and management) practices in order to assess the possible locus of UK economic decline as well as the means to reverse this trend (Handy 1987; Ball 1991).

One reflection that emerges from the mirror is that a traditional focus on a single discipline or subject area, either in teaching or research, leads to a narrow or rigid vision which is unhelpful both for solving pressing socio-economic and environmental problems and for developing flexible and broadly skilled graduates suitable to a 'post-Fordian' era (Ainley 1993). A further reflection is that the problems of the 'real' world (as the world beyond academe is commonly described) do not fall neatly into subject-specific boxes, but flow over the edges of the boxes and into unexpected corners. The solutions to these problems may well be found at the boundaries between the subject boxes, emerging out of combining different ingredients in new combinations, as recent advances in biotechnology or artificial intelligence illustrate. Both these reflections have consequences for traditional ways of organizing, developing and creating knowledge within disciplinary boundaries.

Strategies have been developed within higher education and outside it to tackle some of these socio-economic issues. Examples from within higher education include the development of problem-based curricula in medical education, the development of 'Teaching Company' schemes, and the establishment of new vocational curricula, particularly in the new universities. External initiatives include the Enterprise in Higher Education programme supported by the Department of Employment, The Royal Society of Arts 'Education for Capability' project, the creation of the National Partnership Awards for collaboration between industry and higher education and the competence movement driven forward by the National Council for Vocational Qualifications.

Information technology

A second major cause of change arises from technological developments, particularly in the area of information technology. Writers such as Toffler (1970, 1980), Drucker (1989) and Handy (1989) explore the consequences of the information revolution, arguing that the social, economic and personal impact of this revolution is likely to be more far-reaching than either the impact of the agricultural or industrial revolutions of earlier centuries. While redistributions of wealth and power are occurring now as they did in earlier revolutions, there are other consequences which are qualitatively different. For example, information is not consumed like other resources, nor can it be so easily controlled as labour, capital or land. It is peculiarly democratic in that it tends to provide flatter organizational hierarchies, since it both empowers users (Ainley 1993) and requires weak boundaries between knowledge areas for its efficient use. Information is also generative;

more information is produced through groups of people simultaneously using it, developing it and so creating more value from it. The speed at which this new knowledge renders the old obsolete is increasing: the half-life of knowledge in some of the physical sciences is estimated at present as eight years, while in computing science, this is down to five years (van Ginkel 1994).

The impact of technology and the explosion of information on subjects and disciplines has many facets. In research, the ability to remain at the cutting edge of disciplinary developments has necessarily involved a narrower and ever more specialized focus, particularly in the natural and technological sciences. In the Arts and Humanities, technological developments have increased access to documentary sources or have enabled new creative forms to be developed. In teaching, information technology has created new kinds of teaching materials (screen- rather than text-based), has permitted access to knowledge to be organized differently and has created development opportunities for assessment and evaluation practices in teaching and learning. Technology has also facilitated international exchanges of ideas to the benefit of both teaching and research.

As academic enquiry has become more specialized and more narrowly focused, the disciplines have become more fragmented, new areas mushrooming in previously unified subjects. The burden on students has also increased, particularly in subjects where new knowledge has been added to existing curricula without any change in the traditional coverage expected at different degree levels. The content burden in Physics, Chemistry or Engineering is well recognized (e.g. Doyle and Sparkes 1988; Institute of Physics 1990). In some ways, the dynamic of the information revolution has created a situation in which many academics (novices and initiates alike) are having to run harder and harder in order to stand still, that is, merely to keep up within their subject area.

Technology is also having an impact on the accessibility of knowledge and information. The Open University and open learning opportunities in general are phenomena that have been made possible through technological developments. These developments are also breaking down traditional divisions between home and work as well as between learning and leisure. It is likely that there will be further convergence between these previously separate domains as concepts such as 'the learning organization' or 'learning society' gain momentum (Garratt 1987; Pedler *et al.* 1991; Ball 1992; Duke 1992).

New computing techniques now bring into view the possibility of interactive computer facilities for users in their own homes. Open learning approaches also offer opportunities for private sector companies to offer educational services so reducing the near monopoly of educational institutions. The accessibility of knowledge has the effect of increasing choice for those who want (or can pay) for its acquisition. It is also likely to have the effect of decreasing the traditional power and status attached to the holders of knowledge and information – the academics – and to increase the power of those 'information managers' who are able to help individuals to gain access to the knowledge that they seek.

The widening of choice that technology has assisted in developing extends from choice in the knowledge and information to be acquired to decisions about the place or places in which it will be learned (work, home or college; partly in the UK, partly in mainland Europe) and the time scale and pace at which learning will be undertaken. To accommodate and exploit the potential range of choices made possible through information technology, universities are creating modular curricular structures; they are moving from offering subject-based courses to enabling learning credits to be accumulated by students (through study, work-based learning, practical experience or a mixture of all three); and they are also shifting from a focus on 'reading a subject' to encouraging student learning across a range of academic and transferable skills. The pressure of greater student numbers, the possibilities of IT and developments in the understanding of student learning are combining to make independent and student-centred learning (Entwistle and Ramsden 1983; Brandes and Ginnis 1986; Gibbs 1992; CSUP 1993) a more central feature of higher education.

Beyond economic and technological causes, socio-cultural trends such as the pressure to broaden the range of students entering higher education (to include new socio-economic and cultural groupings and mature entrants, for example) are also working to change traditional curricula to accommodate the diversity of student interest, experience and social origins. Scott and Watson have drawn attention, for example, to the potential for 'feminization and Europeanization' of the curriculum in the future. And finally, post-modernist movements which place emphasis on individualism, relativism and self-determination, and which challenge existing knowledge paradigms, are also influencing curricular changes, particularly in some subject areas such as English and modern languages. Together, these various influences are a further cause of fragmentation in subjects and disciplines, this time as much through developments in teaching as in developments in research.

Changing patterns of intellectual enquiry

Our discussion so far has already drawn attention to shifts within subject areas. Some of these shifts involve changes in teaching and learning structures, for example, modular course structures, accelerated degrees, or mixed-mode learning; others involve changes in content, learning activities or assessment, for example, a lessening of emphasis on disciplinary content and an increasing emphasis on 'process skills' such as teamwork, presentation, communication, or decision-making; on peer-group teaching and computer-assisted learning programmes; on multiple-choice tests, self-assessment tasks or student portfolios of work.

In some cases these shifts have been made through negotiations between staff and students, while in others they have been promoted by groups such as Enterprise teams, employers, educational development units, institutional managers or professional and subject associations. In combination, these various pressures and changes have led to questions about the comparability of standards within subjects (across institutions) and to questions about the boundaries between different levels of academic qualification, from diplomas to doctorates.

In the field of research, there have also been changes. One of these, namely the narrowing of focus and specialization required of researchers who are engaged at the forefront of their subject, has already been mentioned. Others have been driven by different pressures, for example, the increase in contract and applied research (encouraged by financial pressures, by the requirements of vocational curricula, by the need for closer cooperation and communication between higher education and industry, and by new funding methodologies). A further important pressure has arisen out of changes in the size of the higher education system and in the allocation of state funds to universities. From 1987, the funding of research and teaching has been separated, each category of funding now also being linked to judgements of quality. With the move to a post-binary system, there has also been a commensurate increase in the numbers of institutions seeking research support from the Funding Councils; this support is necessarily more thinly spread.

These pressures and shifts have consequences for subject areas and disciplines. Different forms of research (basic or applied) may lead to the development of different research methodologies, are likely to be conducted within different timescales, may result in different contractual arrangements for staff, and ultimately, may be concentrated in different institutions. The impact of these changes in research is filtered through publications, conference presentations, learned societies and consultancy and may involve a relatively slow feedback loop to the fundamental structures of subjects and disciplines. Consequences will also vary across disciplines and across institutions.

Some of the longer-term consequences are likely to include a greater separation of teaching and research and more emphasis on scholarship, as a necessary bridge between the two and perhaps as a proxy for research in some cases. Direct and symbiotic relationships between research and curricula become more tenuous; subjects and disciplines become more instrumental and less curiosity-driven or open-ended in their focus; the boundaries between subjects become increasingly blurred; and subjects may become redefined to reflect the broader, more shallow and messier knowledge that emerges from applied, developmental or action-research compared with the narrower, deeper and 'purer' knowledge that emerges from basic research.

Knowledge may well be differently organized in future (with staff groups stratified accordingly) perhaps to reflect the four areas of 'scholarship' represented in the Carnegie Report (Boyer 1990): the scholarship of discovery, which is most closely related to research at the cutting-edge of a subject; the scholarship of integration which involves synthesizing the results of research within disciplines and creating new knowledge through novel conceptual formulations across subjects; the scholarship of application which involves a deeper analysis of the relationship of theory to practice and the development of a more refined conceptualization of professional practice; and the scholarship of teaching which is concerned with disseminating knowledge and promoting its understanding and its application in many different fields. The Carnegie classification is useful both in highlighting the need for a broader definition of scholarship and in offering legitimacy and recognition to different kinds of academic activity. The important questions are the relative weighting (in terms of time and status) given to each of these activities within and across institutions and the impact that they will have on traditional ways of organizing research, teaching and learning.

Purposes of a subject-based knowledge framework

The changes that we have been outlining can be explored further by reflecting on the purposes that have been served by organizing knowledge within a framework of subjects and disciplines. We can then examine how these purposes may be under threat.

Traditionally, discipline structures have provided a method of presenting knowledge to students, have offered a means of separating truth from falsehood and have provided a way of organizing and coordinating the search for new knowledge. Within universities, teaching and research have usually been organized within departments which are themselves formed around a discipline base. At a deeper level, disciplines and subjects have provided a means of ordering and controlling an otherwise chaotic or irrational physical and social world. They have also stimulated a variety of ways of interpreting, explaining and understanding reality, which are also dynamic and generative, and have encouraged or attracted different modes of thought linked to different intellectual and practical endeavours (Becher 1989).

Social functions are also served in that disciplines provide a common language and means of communication which is internationally recognized; they offer a cultural and often professional identity to those who have been educated within their territory, as well as a source of power, status and authority. Finally, they inculcate values and codes of practice which are of use within the academic world as well as outside it. These varied purposes and functions can, however, have positive and negative implications. For example, the methodological and conceptual framework of a discipline can provide a pathway to cognitive transformations in individuals, but these same frameworks may also constrain thought, making individuals who have been trained within a particular discipline, prisoners within this intellectual paradigm. Between disciplines and subjects, hierarchies can develop which may be harmful economically or socially. For example, the lower status of engineers and educationists in the UK compared with Germany is negative, yet the high value attached to the purer physical sciences may be of positive benefit both to individuals and to society.

Impacts on academic life

Many of the traditional purposes and functions that have been served through the organization of knowledge in a framework based on subjects are threatened either deliberately or unintentionally as a result of the changes we have been identifying. The impact on academic life in general and on individuals in particular – academics, students, academic support staff and managers – is widespread and potentially revolutionary.

At a meta-level, the relationship between the state, the wider society and higher education is shifting. We have argued elsewhere (Barnett and Middlehurst 1993) that this relationship can be represented in four models which, although distinct, have overlaps between them. These four models illustrate the changing patterns of higher education–society relations over time.

The first model, *Higher Education as Private Interest* which was the prevailing model for the nineteenth and much of the twentieth centuries, reflects a position in which the form and practices of higher education were largely a matter of the internal or private interests of the academic community. In this model, subjects and disciplines evolved largely in response to the interests and interactions of academics and in relation to their conceptions of the world at large. Teaching and research were strongly interrelated and control of the curriculum rested with individual academics. The student experience could be conceived as a rite of passage into a particular form of life and mode of thinking, part academic, part social and only incidentally economic. Disciplinary knowledge and understanding, which involved sustained intellectual effort over time, was a primary source of motivation and professional identity for academics. The pursuit of knowledge for its own sake was a hallmark of academic and student engagement in higher learning; and a belief that students and academics were occupied as members of a (disciplinary) community in similar intellectual journeys was part of the prevailing value system. A further important belief, if not always of practice, was that these journeys involved continuous critical reflection about their direction and ultimate destinations.

The second form, *Higher Education as Public Interest* reveals closer attention by the state in the performance of higher education. The last quarter of the twentieth century has seen this model rise to prominence. Here, teaching and research are separated for accountability purposes and in response to economic pressures, and teaching is systematized into courses and programmes which carry some degree of public shape rather than simply being loosely floating intentions in the minds of lecturers. Programmes are still anchored to subjects and disciplines, but the student experience is more instrumental, no longer being conceived largely as an apprenticeship for academic life or an initiation into disciplinary tenets and modes of enquiry. Control of the curriculum still rests with academics, but ownership is more collective than individual, and course leaders and departmental Heads or Deans have some managerial responsibility for the design and delivery of programmes. A sense of community is maintained through the social and organizational unit of the department and through 'professional' identities which are still nurtured largely through subjects and disciplines.

As the funding sources for teaching and research have diverged, so the activities themselves are diverging in order to maximize performance through separate concentration in each area. Departments, which are becoming cost and revenue centres, are changing from predominantly academic entities (loose networks of individual specialists) to more tightly controlled business units. Heads of Departments are acquiring increasing responsibilities for human and financial resource management; through their interventions, academic staff are being encouraged to specialize (in the direction of teaching or research, for example) in order to play to their strengths and to make resource and activity planning and accounting more straightforward. Commitment towards the advancement of knowledge in a subject still exists among academic staff, but other pressures also vie for attention and commitment: research contracts and research-based publications which are more short-term and applied, geared to the demands of the contractor and undertaken more to generate income than to develop the discipline; consultancy contracts which enhance departmental or personal budgets; and management responsibilities which may enhance career prospects but may potentially damage academic progress in furthering a subject or discipline. At the same time, accountability and competitive pressures on institutions have encouraged the development of corporatism. Loyalty to the institution is expected to take precedence over academic commitments to subjects and professions.

Our third form of state–society–higher education relationship, *Higher Education as Public Direction* represents active intervention by the state in the internal character of academic life. It is a feature of late twentieth-century Britain. Research programmes are influenced by public classifications ('strategic' or 'applied' research, for example) since resources are channelled differently according to these classifications and because research capability is affected by the levels of resourcing that are achieved. Research may be still more directly steered where strategic needs are identified by the state or other outside interests and where academic effort is channelled into meeting these needs. The 1993 Science White Paper *Realising Our Potential* is an illustration of Government steerage in its advocacy of 'wealth-creation' as a primary motive in the funding of Science, and in its encouragement of 'useful and relevant' education at Master's and postgraduate level. The acquisition of knowledge for its own sake is significantly downgraded.

Just as research can be steered, so the curriculum can be shaped in response to external interests. In its present guise, this kind of direction takes the form of state sponsorship of particular initiatives (for example, 'Enterprise in Higher Education'), but with the advent of 'mass' higher education as well as other changes mentioned above, state direction might be presented still more overtly, perhaps, in the shape of a 'national curriculum' for the first and second years of undergraduate education. A curriculum of this kind might include the development of civil and community virtues for a multi-ethnic society, enterprising and transferable capabilities to meet the requirements of a changing and competitive economic environment, or computing and linguistic skills to match the future socioeconomic needs of Europe.

The consequences for the development of subjects and disciplines can already be seen. In designing curricula or research projects which match external agendas, the scope for subject development, promoted through the curiosity of academics and involving open-ended enquiry for its own sake, is restricted. Both academic and student identities are affected. For academics, research and teaching are further separated and while internal academic reputation and status is still weighted in the direction of the former, a degree of alienation is likely to emerge between researchers and teachers. Teachers are likely to feel 'deskilled' and devalued since the scope to determine their own curricular goals is curtailed and because they are further removed from the routes to status and academic advancement. Researchers are also differentiated between those who are income generators and project directors and those who are low-waged, short-term contract researchers. The former are often high ranking academics, the latter may not even be full 'academics' (that is, accorded membership and rights within the academic community), being classified instead as academic-related staff. With the advent of larger student numbers, other 'lowly' categories of staff are also being added to institutional ranks in the form of postgraduate and other teaching assistants.

For students, the experience of studying within this model involves an acquisition of knowledge and skills with a primary focus on their practical application and economic return. The danger of an over-prescriptive and essentially closed curriculum is manifest. A more serious threat is that students will miss out both on their independent quest towards enlightenment and on their initiation into the nature of critical enquiry. Where their learning experience has brought them into contact with definitive answers (in the form of a prescribed curriculum) they may not be prepared for the complexity and uncertainty of the world outside higher education. This, of course, is a paradoxical position for the new curriculum to be moving into; the traditional questioning approach to knowledge fostered by academic norms and values in the context of subjects and disciplines may in fact be more appropriate for tomorrow's world.

In our fourth model, *Higher Education as Market Direction*, which is also a late twentieth-century phenomenon, the state relinquishes its close control over the curriculum, the predominant forces for steerage and direction being supplied by 'the market' which consists mainly of students and their employers (whether at graduate, postgraduate or professional development levels). Where research is also market driven, the consequences for state steerage will be similar. However, a significant proportion of research monies (80 per cent plus – see Williams 1992) are still provided by the state through the research councils or through government departments, so that steerage by the state rather than the market is still present.

The drift from state to market direction is both an outcome of Government policy and a consequence of the move from an élite to a mass higher education system. Research is affected since proportionately many more resources need to be directed towards the teaching and learning effort. Teaching is also affected since the volume of throughput of students (particularly when associated with declining unit costs) and the imperatives of institutional competition and positioning mean that management of the curriculum takes on a new significance at all levels of the institution (see King's argument in Chapter 4). As we described earlier, providing an opportunity for student choice which is essential to a market focus, means that the curriculum becomes unitized and learner-based, for example into modules and transportable learning credits. Interpretation of the market and its requirements becomes a matter also of management (and student) judgement rather than being the sole concern of academics.

Some of the potential effects on academics and on subjects mentioned in the third model are reinforced in the fourth model. Teaching is likely to become further dissociated from research and new definitions of research are likely to be developed (perhaps following the Carnegie model, above). The capacity of academics to be involved in knowledge creation is limited since much of their time is now spent in orchestrating learning programmes. These programmes will also need to rely more on the skills of other groups of staff, for example, those information specialists in libraries, computing or audio-visual departments who are not always categorized as academic staff. Not only will other groups of staff need to be involved in curriculum development; students and their employers will also increasingly exert their claims on the content, process, pedagogical relationships and outcomes of the curriculum.

The character of teaching is thus altered from the imparting of a corpus of knowledge and disciplinary methodology to the facilitation of learning and the management and delivery of a negotiated curriculum. Notions of learning are also changing from student formation and induction into a subject area to student acquisition of packages of knowledge (which will need to be regularly up-dated) in combination with a range of transferable skills. The early stages of higher education are no longer assumed to provide a sufficient basis for a student's future: continuous learning and further education will be necessary, undertaken both within a university environment and outside it.

As the organization of the curriculum changes, so academic organization changes in parallel. The delivery of teaching through a subject focus moves first to delivery around a course of study and then to the provision of modules of learning which can be accumulated as learning credits. Similarly, the organization of teaching in departments gives way to its organization within integrated academic frameworks to meet the needs of different student pathways. Relatively open-ended intellectual enquiry engaged in within a disciplinary framework is exchanged for more tightly prescribed outcomes in a range of subject combinations. In terms of teaching and learning, academic coherence, serious engagement within a subject area and a deep level of understanding of disciplinary modes of enquiry are all potentially threatened. And beyond these lie the perceived threats to social and intellectual values of identity, community and territory that were part of the traditional functions and modes of academic organization represented by disciplines and subjects.

Management and staff relationships

The picture that we have tried to paint in this chapter is one in which a number of different forces are converging. These forces are already creating shifts in the traditional character and ordering of university life and they have the potential to create changes of even greater significance which touch many levels of academe, from the conceptual (the idea and purposes of a university), through the operational (policy, structures, systems and activities) to the normative (values, attitudes, beliefs and culture). While these forces and the changes that they are producing are general to higher education in the UK – but are not unique to higher education (Pollitt 1990; Willcocks and Harrow 1992) – the precise shape and pace of institutional and individual response differs across the system, across disciplines and within each university.

In each domain of university life (conceptual, operational and normative) two fundamental processes – communication and relationships – are also affected by the current changes. These two are particularly important since they provide both the evidence of change and the means by which change can be promoted and encouraged, or blocked. In this book, the central focus is on the relationships and communication between academics and managers (or more broadly on those who deliver or manage the curriculum), but as we have suggested, one of the main features of current change is the increasing range of communication and relationships that universities and their members are involved in: with students, their parents, sponsors and employers; with government, commerce, industry and their associated agents; with professional and accrediting bodies. The boundaries of the university are becoming more fluid and more permeable.

This broadening range of recognized higher education stakeholders has had an impact on the time available for academic work (since the networking, lobbying and reporting involved in relationship-building and communication are time-consuming activities). In many cases, the responsibility for undertaking these activities has been channelled to new categories of staff, that is to managers at various levels within the institution. Separating academics from direct contact with stakeholders means that the level of understanding and appreciation of stakeholder interests may reside more with managers than with academics, a point that is important when trying to implement changes in curricula which must be put in place by academics and which rely on academic commitment for their success. A premium is placed on effective communication between management and staff. An additional strategy would be to increase the opportunities for direct communication between academics and other groups (for example, employers) by developing opportunities for secondments, visits and 'curriculum exchange networks'.

Traditional forms of interaction have also been affected by the widening band of stakeholders. For example, accountability and marketing requirements have increased the bureaucratic aspects of communication (to include glossy brochures or video-tapes as well as dense statements of institutional quality assurance arrangements) and mass higher education has reduced face-to-face contact between teachers and students while increasing the interaction between students and technological forms of communication. New terms, and even languages, are emerging as day-to-day currency in institutions, for example: performance indicators; the student-learning experience; customer-care; out-sourcing of services; franchising; competences and portable credits; quality audit; and lecturers as 'facilitators of learning'. Both because of the variety of audiences now involved and because of the increasing scale and scope of higher education operations, the nature of much communication and the style of relationships between higher education and the outside world has moved from the informal and implicit to the formal and explicit. This shift is also evident within institutions and is epitomized in relationships between academic staff and management. A dangerous consequence of more formalized, less direct and often less frequent forms of communication lies in the potential for misunderstanding and misconception between groups within and outside universities.

At the beginning of this chapter, two claims were made: first, that change was perceived as predominantly externally driven and second, that disciplines and subjects represented the academic heartland of universities. It is in the relationships and communication processes between staff and management that these claims are made manifest; and it is these two areas that are of central importance if internal and external perspectives are to be aligned through an effective change management process in higher education.

The many shifts that are being experienced within universities are having a direct impact on the nature of staff roles. As we have already noted, managerial roles have increased in number and the management component of academic roles has also expanded at several levels (Middlehurst 1993). To these we can add the changes that are likely to emerge in the roles of academic support staff as they become more significant players in the facilitation of student learning.

While in some cases an expansion of traditional roles has been occurring, in other cases a splitting of traditional roles is also happening, for example between teaching and research, and between both of these academic activities and management. As roles are separated, they are likely to become more clearly specialized and bounded, so that fluidity across the boundaries is reduced. In practice this means that the skills and knowledge required in each area may become refined to the extent that it is difficult to cross from one area to the other. More rigid boundaries may also reduce levels of communication and contacts between groups as discourse differs, areas of interest and responsibility differ, as timescales and pressures differ, and as status and the value attached to each activity differs. There is a consequent and perceptible effect on relationships between groups.

We have already examined changes in academic roles in relation to subjects and disciplines (for example, separation between teaching and research or the impact of student-centred learning and of mass higher education). At this point we need only highlight the impact of changes in academic roles as they relate to our claims about the academic heartland. The connection lies in the area of motivation since a primary and traditional source of motivation for academics has been the development of their subject area through engagement in teaching, research, scholarship and consultancy. Professional identity, pride, reputation, autonomy and a particular lifestyle are all wrapped up under this heading. Even academics' contribution to administration, within a collegial ethic, was undertaken as a service to the full disciplinary community, that is 'the university', in the interests of self-governance and autonomous control of the affairs of the university, and most particularly, the institution's academic activities. In the former polytechnics, academic involvement in course administration which included close relationships with students created a slightly different kind of 'academic intimacy', but it was no less a source of group and personal identity.

The current changes are encroaching on the academic heartland (Halsey 1992), since shifts in the organization of subjects and disciplines not only affect the core of university activities but also affect the *raison d'être* of many academic staff. Academic staff have observed the rise of a management cadre, the ascendancy of management values and priorities into administrative and financial territories (represented in public reports such as Jarratt 1985, and by financial pressures on institutions) and more recently into the area of the curriculum. They have experienced the demands made upon academic activities – from reorganization, to redefinitions and numerous evaluations – by management. The responsibility for pushing change, while being widely accepted as external, driven by political and economic agendas, is also charged to 'Management'. Institutional managers, in not resisting the encroachments of state or market, are often viewed as the agents of these external priorities, not least because many of the changes have both stimulated management interest and have expanded the scope and status of management activity within the institution.

From a management perspective, the interpretation of the demands and pressures of the external environment may be seen as more or less positive, as more or less necessary and as more or less negotiable between the different interests of providers, consumers and sponsors of higher education. Where the nature and the direction of changes are viewed favourably by institutional managers, responses to implementation can again vary, for example, from treating academic staff as recalcitrant in the face of change, as traditional and unresponsive, as a resource that needs to be controlled and directed for the sake of institutional positioning and effective functioning, or as important partners in the change process. Approaches to the management of change in universities, whether undertaken within a framework of positive or negative attitudes towards academic perspectives, is also hampered by a shortage of resources to facilitate the process.

To polarize academic and managerial perspectives in this way is doubtless to exaggerate the true picture. Interpretations of current changes will vary, many academics and managers sharing common perspectives. Also, there may not be as sharp a distinction as we have made between 'internal' and 'external' views of university activities and of subjects and disciplines in particular. Internal constituencies may welcome many aspects of new curricular or research initiatives while some external interests will be concerned about proposed changes (for example, employers' concern about changes in the classification of degrees – *The Times Higher Education Supplement*, 2 July 1993, p. 2). We have chosen to paint the extremes, partly to draw out the areas of potential conflict and partly to highlight the very real issues that are brought to the attention of unions, personnel officers, staff developers or researchers and consultants concerned with higher education during this period of change. Too often, relationships and communication between academic staff and managers appear to be unidirectional (from management to staff), formal and bounded (approached as consultative rather than participative exercises), and non-negotiable except on clear transactional bases (labour exchanged for a certain level of financial return) (Burns 1978; Bass 1985). Opportunities for creative problem-solving, mutual learning, the development of common interest and shared meaning are thus missed.

Managing change

Stratification within academic institutions is nothing new (Halsey and Trow 1971; Moodie and Eustace 1974) but the particular form that is currently emerging is different, largely because of the managerial and entrepreneurial elements in the present context. Tensions between different groups within the institution are also no novelty, as depictions of the university as a political organization illustrate (see Baldridge 1971). However, these already present features are exacerbated in the present context of change, as individuals feel either threatened or encouraged by the prospects ahead of them.

At a time of public sector resource constraint and during a period when universities have become increasingly dependent on state funds (Tapper and Salter 1992) it is easy to assume that there is little freedom for internal manoeuvre in the approach to the changes that are in train (Russell 1993). Yet, as legally autonomous institutions, universities retain certain freedoms in their organization and management arrangements and in their academic practices. In order to achieve and maintain financial viability and academic credibility, universities can, in large part, determine the most effective ways in which to deploy their resources in line with their declared aims. Given this degree of freedom, we suggest there are at least four strategies that can be used to approach change more constructively as it affects the academic heartland within universities.

A starting point for institutions facing the kind of far-reaching changes that we have been discussing must be the development of a shared interpretation of the nature and extent of the changes facing them. Participation in this debate will both assist the development of an appropriate strategy and will begin the process of building commitment to its implementation. Most importantly, the impact of change on every level of institutional activity can be considered and discussed so that pitfalls are identified early and their consequences for individuals and groups avoided or mitigated. A broad and open debate allows for a proactive and holistic approach to change to be adopted, rather than a reactive and piecemeal stance which runs the risk of permitting unintended (and unwished for) consequences to be visited upon the institution and its members. The different approaches to reductions in funding of the University of Salford and Cardiff University College in the 1980s (Sizer 1987; Shattock 1988) provide examples of some more or less successful approaches to the development of a collective interpretation of change and a strategy to manage it.

Building a view of the external environment, the present position of the institution and its immediate and longer-term priorities, creates a framework for understanding the personal and professional impact of change. Understanding the context and the consequences of change, through discussion and negotiation between key stakeholders, is a necessary prerequisite to identifying a strategy for managing 'change', whether that strategy involves a restatement of present strengths and a commitment to maintaining them, or a more radical shift in direction. Too often, these two elements do not come together: to put it starkly, managers appear to pay most attention to the context and the present position of the institution, perhaps since they have easier access to the information that enables them to develop this perspective as well as a specific responsibility for considering these facets of the situation. Staff (and students) are more likely to concentrate on the personal and professional consequences of change, since they have a direct interest in and access to these kinds of data. The two aspects need to be brought together for effective policymaking and policy implementation to occur.

A fuller understanding of the context and consequences of change is likely to improve internal commitment to change, while negotiation with key stakeholders will develop a level of external trust in the institution's responsiveness to change. Although understanding and trust by themselves will not lead to a commitment to change, they are necessary staging posts along the way.

A second important strategy is to enable those individuals who are most directly affected by the changes (in this case, different staff groups and students) to shape their own operational response to them, within an overall framework. For example, some institutions have been able to introduce controversial changes (such as appraisal of staff performance, student feedback on teaching or the development of teaching and learning compacts) with a minimum of conflict by allowing freedom to design the details of each scheme within general guidelines. Personal involvement creates interest in and 'ownership' of the problem, generates intellectual challenge, stimulates teamwork and will enable professional concerns to be addressed directly. The solutions generated are likely to be more relevant and appropriate than solutions generated by those outside the operational group.

A third strategy is to ensure that the reward systems of the institution and the messages and style of managerial communication are aligned with the changes – conceptual, operational or normative – that are aimed at. If these different elements do not operate in parallel in some degree of harmony with each other, or worse still, contradict each other (as, for example, in promotion criteria which reward research contracts gained or publications achieved when it is changes in teaching that are aimed at), then commitment to change is unlikely to be great and may even be obstructed. A further aspect of alignment is that the rewards, communication and indeed, overall goals of the institution, need to be couched in terms which are both understandable and broadly acceptable to educational and professional concerns in order to avoid alienation of these significant groups.

A fourth strategy, and one that is often neglected, is to manage the transition from the present to the future state. In order to do this, resources are required (and may need to be diverted from other activities), particularly in the form of time, since at every stage – interpretation, negotiation, alignment, communication and operational planning for the future state – time is needed to discuss, gain agreement, identify direction and the means of reaching it. Once planning moves to execution, further amounts of staff and management time are needed to allow communication and feedback on problems and on approaches to their resolution. If there is no commitment to 'managing the transition' and no 'migration strategy' at institutional and faculty levels, then commitment to change among those who must implement it is once again likely to be dampened, squandered or diverted into the necessary task of running present activities.

In combination, these four strategies are likely to lead to more productive dialogue, improved relationships and a wider and more-developed understanding of change between managers and professionals. As Scott and Watson point out in Chapters 1 and 2, a constructive climate is essential if intellectual creativity is to be channelled into new definitions of the curriculum and if 'myopic and Philistine' reforms, imposed by managers divorced from academic concerns, are to be avoided. The positive and exciting educational possibilities of present changes in the subject (and the curriculum more broadly) must not be lost by exchanging 'donnish dominion' for 'managerial rule'. While a new and wider balance of voices is necessary in the shaping of the university curriculum for the twenty-first century, the debate needs to be articulated with educational priorities at the forefront. Management skills and tools are required to support and develop, and not to stifle or control, either the debate or the emerging priorities.

References

Ainley, P. (1993) *Class and Skill: Changing divisions of knowledge and labour.* Cassell, London.

Baldridge, J. (1971) *Power and Conflict in the University.* John Wiley, New York.

Ball, Sir C. (1991) *Learning Pays: the role of postcompulsory education and training.* Royal Society of Arts, London.

Ball, Sir C. (1992) The learning society, *Royal Society of Arts Journal,* 140(5429) 380–90.

Barnett, R. and Middlehurst, R. The lost profession, *European Journal of Education* (forthcoming).

Bass, B. (1985) *Leadership and Performance Beyond Expectations.* Free Press, New York.

Becher, T. (1989) *Academic Tribes and Territories.* Open University Press, Milton Keynes.

Beckhard, R. and Pritchard, W. (1992) *Changing the Essence: the art of creating and leading fundamental change in organizations.* Jossey-Bass, San Francisco.

Bourdieu, P. and Passeron, J.C. (1979) *The Inheritors: French students and their relation to culture.* University of Chicago Press, London.

Boyer, E. (1990) *Scholarship Revisited.* Carnegie Foundation, New Jersey.

Brandes, D. and Ginnis, P. (1986) *A Guide to Student-Centred Learning.* Blackwell, Oxford.

Burns, J.M. (1978) *Leadership.* Harper & Row, New York.

CSUP (Committee of Scottish University Principals) (1993) *Teaching and Learning in an Expanding Higher Education System.* Scottish Funding Council, Edinburgh.

Doyle, S. and Sparkes, B. (1988) *Information Technology For You.* Hutchinson, London.

Drucker, P. (1989) *The New Realities.* Mandarin, London.

Duke, C. (1992) *The Learning University.* Open University Press, Buckingham.

Entwistle, N. and Ramsden, P. (1983) *Understanding Student Learning.* Croom Helm, London.

Garratt, B. (1987) *The Learning Organisation.* Fontana Collins, London.

Gibbs, G. (1992) *Improving the Quality of Student Learning.* Technical and Educational Services, Bristol.

van Ginkel, H. (1994) 'University 2050: the organisation of creativity and innovation'. In Paul Hamlyn Foundation, National Commission on Education and The Council for Industry and Higher Education, *Universities in the Twenty-first Century: A Lecture Series.* National Commission on Education, London.

Halsey, A.H. (1992) *Decline of Donnish Dominion.* Oxford University Press, Oxford.

Halsey, A.H. and Trow, M. (1971) *The British Academics.* Faber & Faber, London.

Handy, C. (1987) *The Making of Managers: A Report on Management Education, Training and Development in the USA, West Germany, France, Japan and the UK.* Manpower Services Commission, National Economic Development Council and British Institute of Management. NEDO, London.

Handy, C. (1989) *The Age of Unreason.* Business Books, London.

Institute of Physics (1990) *The Future Pattern of Higher Education in Physics* (Final Report). IOP, Bristol.

Makridakis, S. (1992) Management in the twenty-first century, in Mercer, D. (ed.) *Managing the External Environment: a strategic perspective.* Sage, London.

Middlehurst, R. (1991) *The Changing Roles of University Managers and Leaders: Implications for Preparation and Development* (Summary Report). CVCP Universities' Staff Development and Training Unit, Sheffield.

Middlehurst, R. (1993) *Leading Academics.* Open University Press, Buckingham.

Moodie, G. and Eustace, R. (1974) *Power and Authority in British Universities.* George Allen & Unwin, London.

Office of Science and Technology (OST) (1993) *Realising Our Potential.* London, HMSO.

Pedler, M., Burgoyne, J. and Boydell, T. (1991) *The Learning Company.* McGraw Hill, London.

Peters, T. (1989) *Thriving on Chaos.* Pan, London.

Pollitt, C. (1990) *Managerialism and the Public Services: the Anglo-American Experience.* Blackwell, Oxford.

Rabinow, P. (ed.) (1984) *The Foucault Reader.* Penguin, London.

Russell, C. (1993) *Academic Freedom.* Routledge, London.

Shattock, M. (1988) Financial management in universities: the lessons from University College, Cardiff, in *Financial Accountability and Management in Governments, Public Services and Charities,* 4(2), 99–112.

Sizer, J. (1987) *Institutional Responses to Financial Reductions in the University Sector, Final Report to the Department of Education and Science.* DES, London.

Sparrow, O. (1993) *Future Scenarios for Britain.* Shell, London.

Tapper, T. and Salter, B. (1992) *Oxford, Cambridge and the Changing Idea of a University.* Open University Press, Buckingham.

Toffler, A. (1970) *Future Shock.* Bodley Head, London.

Toffler, A. (1980) *The Third Wave.* Pan, London.

Wiener, M. (1985) *English Culture and the Decline of the Industrial Spirit.* Penguin, London.

Willcocks, L. and Harrow, J. (eds) (1992) *Rediscovering Public Services Management.* McGraw Hill, London.

Williams, G. (1992) *Changing Patterns of Finance in Higher Education.* Open University Press, Buckingham.

Part 2

Managing the University:
Institutional Heads

4

The Institutional Compact

Roger King

Introduction

This chapter is written from the perspective of the head of an institution which has experienced recently probably more changes than most others in higher education in the UK. From college of higher education to polytechnic and, now, university within less than three years would be change enough in most other eras, but when it is accompanied by incorporation and a growth rate broadly twice as fast as that of the sector norm, then one can but admire the sheer resilience and adaptability of staff and students in circumstances that would have taxed the best private sector companies. However, it is unlikely that the need for efficiency gains will diminish and we have reached the point where a new 'compact' between institutional leaders and staff will need to be forged to manage successfully the changes that will be needed. Broadly, this must be based on the view that current methods of learning have reached the stage where further efficiency exploitation is both unlikely and undesirable, and that a more corporate arrangement of the curriculum, and appropriate resourcing, is needed for reducing the load and consequent stress on staff.

External environment

The external environment that confronts leaders in higher education institutions for the rest of the 1990s looks largely predictable, and has been cogently outlined by Peter Scott and David Watson in Chapter 2. Amongst the key features are:

- growth in student numbers, at least in line with current Government projections of a 50 per cent increase within this decade;
- a continued decline in the unit of funding for teaching, with its velocity dependent on an institution's average costs;

- increased selectivity for research funding and with an increased number of universities (old and new) orientated primarily to teaching;
- a higher focus on the need for public and consumer information on institutional performance and quality for both accountability and competitiveness;
- quickening European and international competition, and collaboration, in the search for funds and reputation;
- increased competition from corporate providers of advanced training and further education providers of higher education;
- selective collaboration between universities but few mergers.

A prime task for university and college heads will be to secure increased efficiency and effectiveness with higher quotients of legitimacy. By legitimacy is meant at least tacit acceptance by staff that managerial decisions seek to provide for their interests and welfare in the light of prevailing circumstances. Efficiency and effectiveness refer to the less subjective processes of outcomes in line with plans and budgets. Obviously, the two factors may be linked. High levels of managerial and institutional efficiency and effectiveness may reduce the need for high amounts of staff legitimation. More positively, perhaps, employee 'ownership' of key changes in organizations is often regarded by employers as a key prerequisite for their successful implementation. Nonetheless, the level of active corporate change may be less than in private sector companies. Disciplinary or departmental identity can be strong and sustain the view that managers are paid to manage (and teachers to teach), and that good results are to be preferred to full participation.

Curriculum

As most institutions in the old polytechnic and college sector have experienced large growth and efficiency gains for several years, the search for at least more of the same will become increasingly difficult without a wholesale consideration of current approaches. There is now little scope for further exploitation of traditional methods (even higher staff:student ratios), or major cost-cutting and rationalization in non-curriculum areas (accommodation, services), without agreement on new forms of learning and how central interventions may be the price for enhanced investment and development. *Managing the University Curriculum* is an apt title for this book because the curriculum will be increasingly managed in the sense that it will more directly come within the compass of the managerial function. But the managed change of the curriculum, as it enters sacred ground, will require higher levels of professional acceptance for it to be successful than was required for those changes that leave the curriculum largely untouched.

It is an interesting, and perhaps remarkable, fact that in higher education the core of the academic enterprise (the course or programme as 'product') lies largely outside corporate control. In the private sector, for example, the product is clearly a matter for senior authorization and monitoring. In universities and colleges the nature and type of courses and programmes (curriculum, structure and delivery) are largely regarded as matters for individual and collegiate regulation. Normative internalization (profession, discipline) and peer processes (validation, review, audit), rather than managerial authorization, provide the accountability and safeguards on behalf of the organization, the public and the consumer. Of course, the allocation of the resources necessary for the provision of programmes is within the managerial domain, but this is viewed as necessarily quite distinct from what is actually provided. The contestability and freedom required for testing, developing and imparting knowledge is traditionally regarded as at odds with managerial interventions.

Our view of the product and how it is constituted is changing rapidly, however. These days it is much less likely to be regarded as a corpus of objective knowledge which, almost incidentally, requires transmission to students. Rather the product encompasses structure, delivery, explicable learning outcomes, flexibility, availability, resourcing and relationship to other products (including a medium or currency of exchange). And the quality of the product is likely to rest more clearly on judgements made by customers and consumers than the producers. It is this wider view of product development, and its evaluation and interrelatedness, that leads to more extensive corporate curiosity in it. The search for growth, efficiency and quality are essential organizational requirements that will take senior managers more directly to the heart of the academic domain.

How threatening or debilitating such intrusions will be for staff will depend on the compact that can be forged with institutional managers. Leaders have to provide the conditions and incentive for the corporate responsibility to be more widely shared – to increase 'ownership' to use the current terminology. But this is much more likely to follow from participation in authoritative and managerially-facilitated task groups than traditional academic collegial forums. Standing committees of Academic Board are not the mechanisms for discussing, agreeing and then implementing decisive and effective product development.

However, managerially focused task groups should seek to incorporate the range of interests and often the mode of collegiality to ensure that professional and academic insights are encouraged. Yet their purpose would be primarily to give programme expression and interpretation to corporate strategy. The direct linkage to senior line management accountabilities not only provides for realistic chances of speedy implementation and adequate appraisal of resourcing, but helps prevent the dangerous divide between directorates that manage resources and academics undertaking the academic enterprise. Vice-Chancellors and senior colleagues must become redirected to the educational heart of their business, but in ways sympathetic and amenable to more decisive corporate action than in the past.

To some extent an uneasy and broadly tacit compact presently exists between management and staff in which the development of courses is agreed as necessary to generate growth and revenue, but that this should not intrude on what was taught and how. Probably it is an agreement that has served the interests of both parties – to date. But as the notion of the product is amplified its development and ability to meet institutional targets generate a need for corporate coordination and wider accountability. Efficiencies needed in the product take it from local and specialist settings and require wider institutional solutions. Such changes are likely to be as unsettling and threatening for 'middle managers' as for lecturers, for they will undermine traditional departmental territorialities and programme control. The basis of departmental and school organizational units could come to look steadily more insecure and permeable. A recasting of schools and departments may identify them as resource centres – human and physical – rather than programme holders. The role for Deans and Heads will be to manage budgets and to ensure the conditions for the professional development of staff, in the light of programme requirements largely generated elsewhere.

Core and foundation curricula

The unitization and modularization of academic programmes in recent years, along with the multi-disciplinarity of provision to be found in the polytechnic and colleges sector, has led to units or courses being available across a number of programmes. For the most part units continue to be owned or offered by schools or departments, but student-centred CATS (Credit Accumulation and Transfer Schemes) are leading to specific cross-institutional and centrally managed programmes. The next key issue will be whether such arrangements provide the basis for an institutional foundation degree curriculum for the early stages of all named degree programmes. That is, will some form of general or core curriculum be developed based on recognizable and general competences as learning outcomes, which, say, all first-year undergraduates would take? It might include, for example, core units in Business, Science, Information Technology methods and Social Science/Humanities. Named degree course routes would become available as part two.

There are a number of advantages to be derived from such an approach:

- Resource efficiency, justifying and allowing considerable investment in learning resources.
- Better-informed choice by students before proceeding to named routes.
- Avoidance of narrow specialization at too early a stage.
- A welcome loosening of tight fit between programmes and specific occupations where this is possible.
- Increased optionality that could be resourced at later stages.
- Ability to focus on explicitly mass forms of higher education in a managed way, i.e. at foundation level.
- Consistent approach to curricula constituted by learning outcomes and competences, and appropriate forms of assessment.

- Avoidance of overloaded curricula and reinforcement of the view that specific forms of occupational training are best provided in employment and supported by continuing professional development.

Clearly, objections can be raised, not least by those staff claiming the inadequacy of the foundation for subsequent specialist study. Yet the benefits could provide the basis for an acceptable and efficient method for both staff and management.

Curricular accountability

Alongside increased unitization and standardization of programmes, and the widening concept of the programme product and its more corporate development, the development of open and resource-based learning will make curriculum materials more visible for comparative evaluation. Lecture notes, handouts and other 'personally owned' and largely secretive media for learning become transformed into public documents whose quality is available for peer, managerial and consumer comparison. Other factors, reinforcing a more public curriculum include:

- An increased emphasis on quality ratings for teaching by government and the Funding Councils whose reputational (as distinct to funding) impact cannot afford to be ignored by institutional managers, particularly where research missions (and therefore research ratings) have been largely eschewed in favour of teaching, and where quality assessment methodology increasingly focuses on teaching and learning and its direct observation.
- Staff appraisal and performance-related pay increasingly linked to teaching performance.
- Extending entitlements for consumers (students) through charters leading to monitoring of services received.
- Consumer-satisfaction constituted notions of quality, alongside peer and producer accounts, requiring the development of wider performance criteria than traditional.
- Greater institutional priority afforded to quality pedagogic and delivery skills in the recruitment and promotion of staff, and the need to monitor and evaluate such skills, and awareness of the necessary specialization of pedagogic skills with the more overt recognition, for example, that a lecture to a large core programme group of around 2,000 students will require particular attributes not possessed by all teachers, and which markedly differ from the more intimate competences required to effectively sustain a successful seminar or tutorial.
- The focus on output as well as input indicators of performance by contractors (especially the Funding Council), and the increased availability of management information systems able to generate higher-grade management surveys and reports.

Learning support

These developments are likely to lead to a further integration of learning resources (library, computing, language and academic support) as will the continued notion of student-centred learning. Whilst the rhetoric of 'independent' or 'student-centred' learning masks a variety of different approaches, what many have in common is a recognition of a move away from overloaded timetables orientated towards formal teaching towards more student learning individually or in groups in libraries, learning resource centres and computer laboratories.

These changes in the provision of learning support are marked by increasing the use of 'non-academic' grades of post such as demonstrators or learning advisors whose primary function is supporting student learning. Institutions have only just begun to think through the staff development and training implications of these new grades of staff. However, even defining them as 'non-academic' staff begins to beg the question about the role and status of academic staff in what will undoubtedly be a 'new order' in teaching and learning. Academics will increasingly have to define themselves as one member of a learning support team, and they may even lose their monopoly over what and how students learn. Increasingly the student curriculum will have to be conceptualized as an institutional responsibility shared by academics and support staff, rather than something to be 'owned' by individual or course teachers. Academic staff's responses to these changes may range from a cautious welcome, to hostility, born out of a fear of exploitation of goodwill by management. The changing role of academic staff in development of new methods of delivery and learning will require planned and sensitive treatment if they are to be committed to the changes.

Suspicion may be increased, however, by the difficult choices that institutions will have to make between increased spending on capital equipment and staffing. Spending on equipment is likely to consume a larger proportion of institutional budgets than previously, with a lower proportionate spend on staffing.

Therefore, higher education institutions are likely to see changes in the balance and ratio of academic and non-academic staff with an increasing emphasis on the role of support staff in course delivery and student learning. These changes will also bring into focus the future of institutional quality assurance systems, with a move away from the predominantly course-based focus towards more holistic approaches taking into account the total quality of the student learning experience.

Accelerated programmes

The notion of a student-centred curriculum makes little sense unless it dispenses with the concept of a 'typical' student with uniform wants, experiences and capabilities. Although this is seen particularly in observed differences between part-time and full-time students, there is little doubt that the pace of progress through programmes and curricula will in the future more reflect the varying needs of so-called mature students. For the most part, progression still largely rests on the premise of the fresh-faced 18-year-old, requiring a wide and residential experience in college life to achieve maturation as well as qualifications.

The introduction of pilot accelerated degrees for mature students, however, reveals that traditional degrees often do not cater for the needs and capabilities and family and related circumstances of mature students, often highly qualified traditionally, who have 'dropped out' of higher education at 18 years of age. For example, at the University of Humberside we commenced an accelerated, two-year degree in Combined Studies for 70 students in September 1993. It is a scheme that rests within the framework for a conventional three-year programme, including the same teachers, external examiners, and so on. Moreover, successful applicants must be at least 23 years of age.

An analysis of applicants reveals a distinct market for such schemes, even if it is likely to remain (and perhaps desirably so) a minority option. To date 61 out of 77 processed applicants are within the age 23–35, with 65 from Yorkshire, Humberside or Lincoln. Moreover, 44 are already in work and 'do not want 22 weeks holiday a year' before returning to the job market. Many have been forced by family or similar circumstances to defer their higher education, but now feel, 'before it is too late', that they have the resource to take a fast-track degree. Only 12 of the 77 were making applications to conventional three-year or part-time courses and the knowledge that they would definitely be working with other mature students was a marked attraction. Nor are they especially non-standard entrants in terms of qualification. A number have three A Levels, highlighting the 'second chance' characteristics of the applicants.

The Monitoring Project on Accelerated Degree programmes, located in the Access and Community Education Service of the University of North London, also has indicated that students on such schemes do have distinctive characteristics supportive of the view that a wider market or source of demand is being reached. In comparison with students on conventional programmes, 88 per cent are mature students (28.1 per cent on parent courses), most are from the locality (70 per cent and 43.7 per cent), there are more with 'non-standard' qualifications (38 per cent and 15 per cent), whilst of those institutions who kept records of students' employment before entry to their courses, 38 per cent were employed (compared with 11 per cent).[1]

There is nothing wrong in students having an instrumental attitude to higher education and its qualifications. If they have other and more personal forms of maturation and leisure, then that is for them. However, the motivation for such accelerated schemes must be market-segment and access based. Although there may be growth and resource payoffs for institutions, it is doubtful in the short-term and cannot be guaranteed in the future. Accelerated programmes are to be justified as meeting needs not currently provided for.

Conclusion: learning resources

In conclusion, corporate curiosity in the learning process is also likely to find expression in the changing role of traditional librarians and other learning support staff. Particularly within the 'new' universities there is increased convergence of library, computer and media services, with the objective of access rather than holdings, and with the aim of support for an independent and empowered end-user. This involves shifts in the balance and responsibility for learning, teaching and support between academics and library and related staff. The latter, rather than passive administrators of resources, increasingly develop proactive learning skills and competences.

A major challenge for institutions will be in helping to redefine the learning responsibilities of lecturers as the organizational convergence of academic and learning support staff is developed to ensure continued efficiency gains. The greater variation in types of students and types of learning will reinforce these tendencies, but also lead to more complex provision. The expansion in networks and databases requires academic and library staff to become gatekeepers and interpreters to informational availability and how they are to be used. Explicit models of learning will be essential for both types of staff, and the distinctions between the types will blur.

It will be essential that corporate strategies for curricula and learning are matched by increased emphasis, and therefore corporate responsibility, for more sophisticated and better resourced human resources policies.

Note

1. *HEFCE's Accelerated and Intensive Routes to Higher Education: Research and Evaluation Project* (1993) ACES, University of North London.

5

Living with Ambiguity: Some Dilemmas of Academic Leadership

David Watson

Introduction

This chapter is not a professional contribution to human resource management, but rather a personal assessment of the effects of some of the pressures identified in previous chapters on the behaviour of senior managers in universities. That said, the current intense interest in higher education of the management studies community is gratifying. There are some highly respectable reasons for their interest. We run extremely complex organizations, with a wide and changeable product mix, on the basis of very flat structures of responsibility for quality and development. We have also met and exceeded targets for dramatically increased productivity, without (apparently) sacrificing quality. (Incidentally, I subscribe to the interpretation that says that quality of *output* has been maintained; what have been lost are some important elements of the quality of *life* within our institutions – for students perhaps even more than for staff.) This leads to a less respectable rationale for higher education institutions as laboratories for management science. For some time now we have supplied the only sector-wide growth industry around.

It is also important to point out that this assessment comes from the chief executive of a higher education corporation (HEC). We are all universities now (at least for the purposes of the UCAS handbook), but we are not all chartered bodies with the illusion of self-governing democracy on the model of late mediæval Bologna. What is a higher education corporation? Who owns it? To whom or what is it accountable? What can its employees, and that particular set of employees which it wishes to call 'managers' legitimately expect, especially against some of the assumptions about 'traditional' university governance? The Chairman of the Board of Governors at the University of Brighton, Michael Aldrich, has some trenchant views about this:

> The HEC concept – exempt charity where the Charity Commissioners have no supervisory powers, where the Secretary of State has some

reserve powers, where the Funding Council can impose conditions and terms on the use of the funds it provides, and where the independent Governors can create independent Governors in perpetuity – has created the MANGO: mostly autonomous national government organisation, an exotic and delicate fruit with unknown side-effects.[1]

At the heart of the MANGO is, of course its Board, wherein all of the key provisions of the Further and Higher Education Act of 1992 – on funding and on degree-awarding powers – are vested. This Board has one executive Director, and no place for a Chancellor, a Vice-Chancellor, or even a Treasurer. Some of the enthusiasm of former members of the Committee of Directors of Polytechnics for the ceremonial trappings of university status will, in due course, come up against these hard facts.

Myths

As HECs, not long liberated from local authority control we have, of course, a particular angle on some of the myths which the higher education enterprise has generated to give itself comfort and security. In a splendid codification of these myths Richard Millard sets out the 'families' listed in Fig. 5.1. In the case of the fundamental seven 'academic sacred cows' which underpin the analysis, we in the higher education corporation have our own special motes and beams. His definitions are as follows: the Golden Era ('veneration of the past and its use as normative for the present'); reform from within ('the only legitimate reform of higher education comes from within the academy'); the traditional College Student ('the "real" . . . students on which we should concentrate are the 18- to 24-year-old resident students'); the centrality of the University ('the university, particularly the research university is the paradigm for all postsecondary education'); the transfer of credit (the restriction of transfer to 'comparable' institutions); the older student ('that older students dilute program quality'); and Continuing Education ('that adult and continuing education programs are primarily either auxiliary money-making enterprises or "public services"').[2]

On some of these the HECs can feel smugly superior. Our 'golden age' was never quite as luxurious as that of the Oxford common room (except in corners of the teacher education world). We were always accountable, to local authorities and to professional bodies. Our students were significantly older, more varied in background, and often part-time. Simultaneously, as Table 1.1 (p. 23) illustrates, it was the polytechnics and colleges (and not the universities) which created the current 'gender neutrality' of UK higher education.

We can, however, get carried away by these differences. Many of the so-called 'traditional' universities (the new term of art from the DfE) have worthy achievements in 'non-traditional' areas, while many of our flexible

Figure 5.1   Richard Millard, *Today's Myths and Tomorrow's Realities* (1991).

1. **'Sacred cows'**
   The Golden Era myth
   The Reform from Within myth
   The Traditional College Student myth
   The Centrality of the University myth
   The Transfer of Credit myth
   The Older Student myth
   The Continuing Education myth

2. **'Turf battles'**
   Autonomy myth
   Competition myth
   State Board myth

3. **'Curriculum'**
   Liberal Arts Contamination myth
   Professional Education Exclusion myth
   Curricular Absolutes myth
   Feet of the Master myth

4. **'Quality'**
   Reputational Input myth
   Research-Publication myth
   Undergraduate Focus myth
   Non-traditional Education myth
   Non-credit Course myth
   Assessment myth

5. **'Equity'**
   Equity vs Quality myth
   Higher Admissions Standards myth
   Remedial Work myth
   Value-added myth

6. **'Educational technology'**
   Sanctity of the Classroom myth
   Threatened Faculty myth
   Collegiate Service Station myth

7. **'Business and industry'**
   Interference myth
   Captive Classroom myth
   In-service Education myth

new structures are more effective in the packaging (modularity, access policies, etc.) than in the content (evidence of genuine widening participation). Perhaps a government-inspired period of consolidation will lead to some systematic owning-up.

Models of leadership

How should our single executive director operate in these circumstances? For one thing, he or she is not short of advice. There exists a rich vein of theorizing about the personality characteristics of successful leaders, of which Fig. 5.2 is an example. This taxonomy, from Amanda Sinclair of the Graduate School of Management of the University of Melbourne, is both persuasive and unnerving.[3] To succeed you have to be all of these things, sometimes simultaneously.

One less benign effect of this type of analysis is that it encourages the cult of personality. We are all familiar with powerful institutional heads who

Figure 5.2   Amanda Sinclair, *Archetypes of Leadership* (1990).

	Stresses
1. Scientific Manager	control accountability
2. System Manager	coordination integration
3. Caring Leader	nurturance devolution
4. Politician/Statesman	coalitions ambassadorial role negotiation
5. Meaning Manager	myths and symbols legitimation
6. Entrepreneur	risks and opportunities initiative
7. Transformative/Visionary	empowerment 'cooperative individualism' vision
8. Moral Guardian	standards community interest concern and caution

have become synonymous with their institutions. In some senses our chief executive of the HEC has too much power. In time many become caricatures of their former, better selves.

This problem – the concentration of power – stems in part from a lack of a clear alternative; the institutions can no longer operate (if they ever could) on the basis of eventual consensus. Speed of change for institutions is probably now a greater challenge than its depth. Woe betide the university unable, or simply unwilling, to analyse and respond to the weekly dispatch box of Funding Council circulars.

It is also hard for senior managers to remember that they are just one of a set of stakeholders in the prosperity, effectiveness and culture of their institutions. They are as much prey as others to another disturbing feature of our contemporary educational scene, which could be termed the *asymmetrical sympathy syndrome.* Each of our stakeholder groups reserves complexity and ambiguity to itself, and regards all other groups in simplistic and caricatured terms. Each group believes it, exclusively, knows what is really going on, and what simple steps could be taken by others to put it right. The moral force of the argument is with it (whether it is the 'academic tradition' of the lecturer's group, or the 'market sensitivity' of the institutional

Figure 5.3 William Empson, *Seven Types of Ambiguity* (1930).

1. Meaning several things simultaneously

    e.g. QUALITY

2. Resolving two or more meanings into one

    e.g. EFFICIENCY

3. Two ideas ... given in one word simultaneously

    e.g. TEACHING

4. Two or more meanings, not agreeing among themselves

    e.g. CHOICE

5. Incomplete performance by the author

    e.g. DIVERSITY

6. Saying nothing

    e.g. MODULARITY

7. Two opposite meanings

    e.g. UNIVERSITY

heads). More damagingly, each group has clear-cut, unambiguous views of the motives and intentions of the other groups, often cynically expressed. Coupled with our collective myth-making propensity – for example, that things were once significantly better (a kind of envy of our former selves), and that net additional resources would solve all of the outstanding problems (often envy of others) – this creates a volatile mixture.

Seven types of ambiguity

What we have to do, whether we celebrate this fact or not (and I will return to the philosophical implications of that question) is to live with complexity and ambiguity. William Empson's *Seven Types of Ambiguity* is the classic study of ambiguity in the creation and reading of texts, and a fruitful source of games outside of the literary sphere. Fig. 5.3 shows his seven types of ambiguity (with their features of 'advancing logical disorder') in the context of current higher education policy and practice.[4]

1. *Meaning several things simultaneously* ('that a word or a grammatical structure is effective in several ways at once'). The best example is probably *quality*. There are at least two major, well-founded research projects trying to resolve what is meant by quality in higher education (at the

Universities of London and Central England). Can it really mean 'fitness *for* purpose' without consideration of 'fitness *of* purpose'?[5]

2. *Resolving two or more meanings into one* ('when two or more meanings are resolved into one'). An example is *efficiency*. What is the 'efficiency' of the higher education process (cheapness, throughput?) without 'effectiveness'?

3. *Two ideas in one word* ('when two ideas, which are connected only by both being relevant in the context, can be given in one word simultaneously'). Note how we have had to accept *teaching* (as in the funding councils' assessment of 'teaching quality') as meaning both teaching and learning.

4. *Two or more meanings, not agreeing among themselves* (as 'evidence of a more complicated state of mind in the author'). This can be seen in the twisting and turning over *choice* (the way in which, for example, student choice became 'informed student choice' in Government pronouncements when it became clear that students preferred to read History to Mechanical Engineering, and note the continued popularity of the former even after a barrage of publicity about the earning potential of the latter). Similar problems are raised by the concept of *competition* in higher education. Our corporation is encouraged to compete as an economic individual (the classic definition of corporation in legal terms) in the marketplace, and yet cooperate in areas like educational technology.

5. *Incomplete thinking by the author* ('when the author is discovering his idea in the act of writing, or not holding it all in his mind at once'). What about the Government injunctions on *diversity*? Is it just another way of saying 'rationalization, but not yet'?

6. *Saying nothing* (so that the 'reader is forced to invent statements of his own'). Diversity would also do here, but what about *modularity*? The buzz word of the 1980s could become the myth of the 1990s, as institutions line up to 'modularize' or to 'semesterize', without any real intention to increase flexibility for students.

7. *Two opposite meanings* (showing 'a fundamental division in the author's mind'). I have already reflected on what might now be meant by the term *university*.

In practical terms, at the sharp end, all of these ambiguities impact in particular ways on the managers and the academic leaders of the institutions. These are some of the things we are required to do.

1. *Strive to do more, better, with less.* Here is another thought from Chairman Aldrich, commenting on the notes of a senior management seminar on resourcing the University of Brighton 'from the perspective of a bemused private sector outsider':

> From that perspective, the central management problem is the economic performance of the production unit. The solutions are straightforward – standardise, rationalise, simplify the products, polish the pearls and dump the dogs, optimise the batch sizes, sweat the assets

on 2¹/₂ shift production [this was before the Flowers Inquiry], invest in products that are more cost-effective to produce and sell, apply appropriate strategies to products depending on life-cycle positioning and so on . . . You would then have a highly efficient and very focused plant. Unfortunately, because you cannot raise capital from share-holders, or debt without artificial limits from banks, you can only pursue sub-optimal strategies.

The higher education sector is in some androgynous state trying to be private sector in operating performance and public sector in control of and access to funds – capitalism without capital or using the techniques without the brass.

The amount of creative brainpower being applied to square the funding circle beggars belief . . . The public doesn't deserve such servants.[6]

2. *Embody and inspire both realism and idealism.*
3. *Balance protection and involvement.* It is difficult to be both a barrier against the unwelcome effects of change and a facilitator of it.
4. *Obey injunctions to compete and to cooperate.*
5. *Achieve step changes in practice and incremental improvements in quality.* Here the precepts of Total Quality Management and 'continuous improvement' run almost directly counter to the pressure for radical review and revision of practice.
6. *Keep confidence of clients and argue for additional investment.*
7. *Is there any such thing as an academic leader?* You might be tempted to think it is yet another oxymoron, 'like enterprise in higher education'. A colleague of mine used his inaugural lecture to press the point:

. . . the letter 'f' in the word professor is at once unexpectedly valuable and insidiously threatened, in so far as the only other single letter in the alphabet which can be substituted for it to make a single word is 'c'. Now I don't think 'professors' should become 'processors' – just as I don't think less elevated lecturers should either – nor that students should be 'processed'; and yet many of the current determinants on higher education in Britain do not give me much hope for retaining the 'f-letter' in place of the 'c' . . .

Let me assure you, this is not a plea for sympathy; I am conscious that higher education has changed fundamentally and irreversibly (often for the good) even over the last dozen years; that it has to be managed; and that people like myself have knowingly taken relatively high salaries to become middle managers in the new companies. Devolved budgets have to be controlled; staff development has to be undertaken; monitoring and evaluation . . . must be seen to be squeaky-clean; Research Selectivity Exercise returns have to be made; spread-sheets are *de rigueur*; Health and Safety, Equal Opportunities, Staff Appraisal, and many other training workshops have to be attended. And so, no doubt, should all this be. It's just that I hear

> the 'Processoriate' coming ominously closer, and I wonder (a) will professing still be part of the job? and (b) will what I profess still be thought worth professing?[7]

Now what is going on here is, I think, both subtle and important, even if we forgive the disclaimed and then reinstated plea for sympathy. At one level it is another 'golden era' case; certainly being a professor and a head of department once was a more relaxed, and in that sense satisfying avocation (so, too, was being a schoolteacher). But was all of the price worth paying? Do not the other individuals in the department – students and staff – deserve a type of leadership (and management) that takes more systematic account of their interests than the occasional glance over the shoulder of the pioneering researcher? Did they get this in the 'golden era', before the current pressure on resources raised the stakes? It seems doubtful.

I attempt below to set out some practical ideas for managers, and for 'the managed', within institutions. These are designed to clarify objectives, to improve practice, but above all to underline and (in some circumstances) restore the common cause of all who work in them. They are not intended to be a counsel of perfection.

1. *Give clear, specific messages about constraints and opportunities.* Avoid the sense of mystery, and/or conspiracy, about the 'management's' assessment of the strategic position of the institution.
2. *Don't oversell either threats or opportunities.* Resist the temptation to attempt to scare, or to bribe, colleagues into the appropriate responses.
3. *Prepare step changes in practice in advance.* Sudden, institution-wide edicts – e.g. 'we shall be modular by September' – rarely work, and often stimulate sophisticated and effective resistance strategies.
4. *Protect the academic infrastructure, even if it means hard choices.* If you let a piece of the infrastructure, say a library collection or a research group, or a curriculum area like teacher education go, you never get it back.
5. *Don't get disengaged from the operation.*

These obviously only work with some reciprocal obligations being met by the other groups within the university. Here are some thoughts for teaching and support staff.

1. *Establish agreed pattern of workload clearly.* One of our starkest lacks, within the university, is an effective and comprehensive mutual understanding of obligations – what Roger King in Chapter 4 calls a 'compact'.
2. *Think about the* purposes *of assessment.* This is perhaps our biggest challenge to practice as the system expands: if you make no changes to assessment, you will spend more time doing it.
3. *Don't feel you have to do it all yourself; build teams.* One of the major morale traps, for teachers especially, is the effect of making major changes alone, and feeling that they are 'letting go' or 'letting the side down'.
4. *Welcome rather than deny responsibility.* Responsibility, for budgetary control or for 'quality', can and should be an asset and not a liability; in particular

it can get you into the strategic planning debate at a different level – with more chances of controlling rather than being controlled by management destiny.

5. *Don't turn the department into a laager.* Team-building goes wider than the department.
6. *Above all, think hard before you invite students (and other clients) to collude in your own frustration.* Remember that they only get one shot at an experience which for us is a career-long privilege.

Contingency, irony and solidarity

I would like to conclude with a thought about the philosophical implications of all of this. It is not intended to be a post-modernist invitation to relativity and value neutrality. On this point, as on several others, I am ultimately with the American philosopher Richard Rorty, who has tried to steer an individually and socially responsible path between philosophical absolutes and fashionable solipsism. To borrow, and oversimplify the theme of one of his most famous books, I think, in work within higher education institutions as well as in life, that we should recognize contingency, celebrate rather than be defeated by irony, and take strength in solidarity.[8]

Notes

1. Personal letter to author.
2. Millard, Richard (1991) *Today's Myths and Tomorrow's Realities: overcoming obstacles to academic leadership in the 21st century*, pp. xiv–xv. Jossey-Bass, San Francisco and Oxford.
3. Sinclair, Amanda, 'Archetypes of Leadership', University of Melbourne Graduate School of Management Working Paper No. 11 (June 1990), p. 16.
4. Empson, William (1956) *Seven Types of Ambiguity*, 3rd edn, pp. 1, 2, 48, 102, 133, 155, 176, 192.
5. Harvey, L. and Green, D. (1993) Defining quality. *Assessment and Evaluation in Higher Education*, 18(1), 9–35.
6. Personal letter to author.
7. Widdowson, Peter (1993) 'Newstories: Fiction, History and the Modern World', University of Brighton Inaugural Lecture.
8. Rorty, Richard (1989) *Contingency, Irony and Solidarity*. Cambridge University Press, Cambridge.

Part 3

Managing the Curriculum:
Middle Managers and Lecturers

6

Educational Development

Dai Hounsell

Introduction

Most universities have some kind of overt organizational framework concerned with sustaining and enhancing the quality of learning and teaching within the institution. This concern with 'educational development', as it is often called, embraces a range of functions such as coordination and oversight of teaching policies and procedures, academic staff training and development, quality assurance, advisory services on learning strategies and study skills, and encouraging and supporting new curriculum, teaching and assessment initiatives. In some universities, most or all of these functions are underpinned by a central agency such as a Teaching, Learning and Assessment Centre, an Educational Development or Educational Methods Unit, or a Centre for Academic Practice, or they are pursued by a cluster of agencies each of which has responsibility for a particular function such as staff development or study guidance to students. Similarly, oversight of educational development may be vested in a single overarching committee or board or range across several such bodies – in either case, usually with parallel structures at the faculty or school level.

None of these structures, it hardly needs saying, is intrinsically better than the other: the particular framework followed, together with the resources allocated to it, is likely to reflect and be attuned to each institution's distinctive organizational ethos and patterns of decision-making. It will also, of course, reflect the relative weight accorded to teaching in the strategic movement of the institution, which has come into much greater prominence – even in some of the most traditional of UK universities – as a consequence of new challenges and demands. Three of the most pressing of these and their implications are considered from the standpoint of education development, for managing the university curriculum in the years ahead:

• Quality and pressures on resources for teaching.
• Quality and shifts in teaching–learning strategies.
• Quality and measures towards greater accountability.

Lastly, the most urgently required strategies for enhancing teaching quality will be reviewed.

Quality and resources

No one working in higher education in recent years can fail to be aware of the problem of resources for teaching: unit costs have been driven down and are projected to fall still further as greater 'efficiency' is seen as the main stratagem for levering in ever-larger numbers of students. Yet, though it is incontestable that resources questions will need to be at the forefront of our thinking about teaching over the rest of the decade, a less muddied view of the issues seems essential.

Call on costs

First, universities are only slowly coming to terms with the fact that – as in other spheres of everyday life, whether in the commercial sector or the public services – expectations of quality continually shift upwards, with the result that new calls are made upon resources which do not hold out straightforward possibilities for matching reductions elsewhere. One example of this is low-tech: in recent years ample handouts, well-crafted overhead transparencies and reliable course documentation have come to be seen as routine accompaniments to a well-taught course. It is therefore no longer possible to see them as discretionary items when course budgets become overstretched, even though there would be a continuing wish to ensure that spending on them was judiciously controlled.

Another example is a high-tech one: computer literacy, which is going to bite harder and harder into funding allocations for teaching. Here again, an institution's freedom of action is limited. It is doubtful whether a few years from now there will be any academic discipline where the provision of high-quality undergraduate education does not entail computer-based learning – or indeed whether students or employers would be attracted to an institution that was not committed to computer literacy at all. Nor, on any hard-headed analysis, should hopes be entertained that computing and information technology will offer an economic means of teaching large classes – whatever it proves necessary to argue on investment grounds to funding bodies. We shall, most likely, simply have to find ways of paying for it.

This situation means rethinking current patterns of expenditure on teaching to accommodate new calls upon resources, and it calls into question the continued appropriateness of relying on such blunt indicators as staff:student ratios when the funding of teaching and learning is contingent upon many different areas of expenditure over and above salary costs. But informed thinking about the resourcing of teaching is not feasible without valid and reliable data on costs, and these are not readily or widely available.

What costs what?

How many institutions, for example, currently know how resources on teaching are deployed? And how many are confident that funds are allocated in a way which means that departments start from similar baselines – once subject-specific needs have been allowed for – in their capacity to resource their teaching commitments? Indeed, is there even an established methodology for actually costing the resources which are allocated to teaching in an acceptable or reasonably accurate way?[1]

In fact, some recent discussion about ways of teaching larger student numbers seems simply to illustrate a less than firm grasp of resource issues. There is talk of building mammoth lecture theatres, when lecturing is an economic – if not wholly effective – method of teaching large groups (see for example Bligh 1972), and when the marginal costs of repeating an already prepared lecture are relatively low. Budgets are kept in check by scrimping on multiple library copies of essential books, where the outlay is comparatively small yet the consequences for the breadth and depth of students' understanding may be far from negligible. At the same time, assessment procedures which call for very considerable investments of staff time and effort seem often to escape scrutiny, while large disparities in tutorial provision persist, within and across institutions, which often seem largely a function of unexamined past practices rather than a direct reflection of differences in staff:student ratios.

Resource and quality questions

From a managerial point of view, however, deploying resources for teaching and learning poses particular difficulties. One is that it is not feasible (and is certainly undesirable) to attempt to review teaching costs in isolation from considerations of quality and especially in isolation from thinking about course aims and learning outcomes. Yet some of the quick-fixes which are apparently being contemplated in some institutions – reading the last rites over small group teaching, pruning the provision of feedback on students' coursework and concentrating efforts on didactic teaching of the largest number of students in the least expensive way – suggest that thinking about means has lost sight of ends. Some loss of 'academic intimacy' as David Watson and Peter Scott put it in Chapter 2, may be inevitable. But without proper consideration about how high-level learning goals are going to be achieved (and lectures, on the available research evidence, are no solution), the quality of students' learning will be put in serious jeopardy.

A second and related difficulty is that imaginative thinking about how to deploy limited teaching resources in more telling ways cannot be left to

financial managers alone. The fundamental issues are much more pedagogical than financial: they call for expertise in teaching–learning methods
and an understanding of the distinctive requirements of different subject
and course settings. Consider, for example, two directions where considerable scope for more cost-effective use of resources exists in ways which
sustain and may even in some cases enhance the quality of learning. (Both
examples are discussed more fully in the section which follows.) One involves
giving students greater responsibility for their own learning (Gibbs and
Jenkins 1992), while the other lies in using computing and information
technology to strengthen study guidance and course management and
administration. Making progress on both these fronts requires an alliance
of expertise: a readiness on the part of the university teachers to work
through the resource implications of educationally desirable initiatives, and
a readiness on the part of those responsible for financial management both
to rethink patterns of resource allocation in the light of shifting teaching–
learning strategies and to invest in educational change.

Quality and teaching – learning strategies

In what ways might we expect teaching and learning strategies (and thus
notions about what counts as quality in teaching) to shift over the next
decade? The most obvious trend is likely to be towards much greater diversity within and between programmes of study, in course design, teaching–
learning methods and assessment procedures. Underlying this trend is a
threefold stimulus: evolving ideas about how to promote high-quality learning; resource-driven pressures to reallocate teaching effort in more imaginative ways; and the seemingly unstoppable gallop towards modularization,
which can foster greater diversity through sharpening internal competition
for students while lessening the need for staff with new initiatives in mind
to run the gauntlet of more traditionally-minded departmental colleagues.

Quality and diversity

Greater pedagogical diversity in itself, of course, may not seem at first glance
an especially glamorous project. And as an example of the 'dangerous'
code which Jean Bocock and David Watson warn of in Chapter 9, it can be
abused: 'anything goes', or 'anything will do' is an obvious hazard. But
appropriate and constructive diversity can be taken as one hallmark of
quality in teaching. It is more stimulating for students than a 'bread-and-
water' diet of lecture, tutorials and end-of-year examinations; it can help to
set intellectual challenges which extend beyond content to the processes of
learning and teaching; and it nudges students towards becoming more
versatile and resourceful learners – a capability which they will need if they
are to go on renewing and updating their knowledge in the years beyond
graduation (Denicolo *et al.* 1992).

Student involvement in learning

Where, specifically, will the main shifts in teaching–learning strategies be found? Some of these, at least, can be picked out with a reasonable degree of confidence. First there are efforts towards involving students more actively in their own learning. These can take many different forms, for example, the following:

• Replacing some conventionally taught courses by self-study materials of various kinds, allied to support mechanisms such as tutorials and efforts to help students to improve their learning strategies and study skills (Rowntree 1990; Cryer and Elton 1992; Entwistle and Tait 1992).
• Encouraging students towards more collaborative learning, whether through a blend of tutor-led and tutorless tutorials, group-based projects or student support networks and self-help groups (Jacques 1984; Griffiths and Partington 1992; Hartley and Bahra 1992).
• Giving students a greater role in evaluating the quality of their own work and other students' work (Boud 1986; Falchikov and Boud 1989; Brown and Pendlebury 1992; Hounsell and Murray 1992).

There is nothing especially new about moves towards greater student involvement in learning, which have been under way in most institutions for some time. Until recently, however, the arguments advanced in their favour, though compelling, were essentially pedagogical: more active student involvement can help to enhance motivation, promote greater intellectual autonomy, encourage students to reflect on and take responsibility for their own learning needs, and lead to higher-quality learning outcomes (Denicolo *et al.* 1992; Entwistle 1992). What has changed, it seems, and has brought about a quickening of pace, is the perception that involving students more fully in the process of teaching and learning can help alleviate constraints on resources, and especially constraints on staff time. A further and perhaps less well-acknowledged influence results from the wider adoption of accountability measures (see below), of which academic audit and quality assessment are the most recent manifestations. More vigorous and more visible top-down encouragement of student-centred teaching is seen as a tangible way of demonstrating a commitment to teaching quality. The complacent view that teaching is essentially a departmental or faculty matter is no longer tenable.

Computer and information technology

A second and equally inexorable shift is in applications of technology – and in particular computing and information technology – to teaching and learning. As indicated earlier, substantial institutional investment in this technology on a progressively larger scale seems unavoidable (as is continued strategic development of the kind represented by the Funding

Councils' Teaching and Learning Technology Programme) to meet rising expectations of what quality in teaching entails. But what will be the most constructive channels for investment in teaching applications? One may be sceptical about the possibilities of this technology for large-group teaching, where more conventional methods of transmitting knowledge and 'covering the syllabus' (printed material and lecturing) will almost certainly have the edge on grounds of cost, except perhaps for packages on topics where there is a large market and a readily identifiable core curriculum (e.g. Mathematics for engineers). We are much more likely to see further growth in the use of the computers as powerful tools to help meet appropriate subject-specific learning requirements, whether through simulation and modelling, computer-aided design, analysis of data-sets and databases, or text processing and revision (see, for example, CSUP 1992: 12–17 and 63–66). But what the impact of the more recent developments such as multimedia will be is still hard to discern; as with all such developments, the prospects are exciting and it is tempting to get starry-eyed about possibilities, but it will take time to root out realistic and apt ways of capitalizing on its potential.

There are also promising avenues which we are only just beginning to open up in exploiting computing and information technology to support various aspects of course management and study support, for example:

1. To disseminate course guides, reading lists, handouts and other teaching and study materials.
2. To exploit the potential of periodicals and other materials now appearing in CD-ROM format as a mainstream resource base for student projects.
3. To record and track students' progress more systematically.
4. To identify high-risk students.
5. To help students to identify and address shortcomings in their study strategies.
6. To give students diagnostic feedback on assignments.
7. To help academic staff to obtain and process course feedback economically, e.g. using optical mark reading technology.[2]

Such applications will be slow to emerge so long as the teaching challenge is seen as the narrow one of 'delivering instruction' rather than as, more fittingly, that of managing a complex and interrelated array of learning opportunities.

Targeted support for learning

Two further, and perhaps less immediately apparent, shifts in direction should also be mentioned. One of these has already been hinted at, if only by implication, and that is better targeting of support of learning. As enrolments continue to rise, student populations are becoming much more sharply differentiated in the knowledge, skills, values and attitudes which they bring to their undergraduate studies. Many of these students, like their predecessors, will arrive adequately equipped for undergraduate study, or at least able to get by; many others will be at risk of underachieving or failing without well-focused and sustained help with learning and study difficulties. In times of plenty and more measured growth, traditional support frameworks (tutorial and counselling systems) could rise to the challenge. Whether they will be able to do so in a period where rapid growth combines with proportionately lower funding is much more doubtful. It may be essential to take a combination of measures to safeguard quality of outcome (i.e. levels of academic achievement as well as retention and qualification rates) including the following:

- Channelling a rather higher proportion of resources into support services and systems (not easy to achieve if we recall that support services have often borne the deepest cuts in periods of recession).
- Attempting a systematic audit of the knowledge and skills of incoming students (rather than waiting for shortcomings to reveal themselves).
- Recognizing the limitations of existing tutorial and counselling systems, which tend to be largely generalist and may therefore need to be strengthened by more specialist expertise (whether to respond to language and writing difficulties, an inadequate grasp of Mathematics or Statistics, large gaps in some students' subject knowledge, or specific needs arising from conditions such as dyslexia).

Accommodating students' aspirations

The other less-obtrusive shift concerns learning aspirations on the part of students which lie beyond their formal programmes of study – at least, as conventionally conceived. These aspirations include the following:

- Learning a new foreign language, or deepening one's mastery of an existing one.
- Acquiring general-purpose computer literacy skills in areas (e.g. document formatting, use of spreadsheets) not necessarily covered in one's chosen subjects.
- Developing personal and transferable skills of the kind currently being pursued under the aegis of Enterprise programmes, with an eye to longer-term career development.

Many such opportunities already exist or are being energetically developed within present higher education curricula, but not all can readily be accommodated within existing course structures in ways that meet student rather than solely institutional concerns. This raises questions for institutions both about the legitimacy and acceptability of students using some of their study time in this way, and about how far formal credit and recognition for learning of this kind can feasibly be stretched. Certainly, institutions' readiness to acknowledge and accommodate such aspirations – what Bocock and

Watson depict in Chapter 9 as 'ownership of the course shifting to the student' – may itself emerge as an index of teaching quality.

Quality and accountability

The last few years have brought stronger formal measures of accountability for quality in teaching and course provision in several countries (see for example, Craft 1992). In the UK, the introduction of academic audit has extended to the traditional universities some aspects of accountability procedures which have long been familiar in polytechnics and colleges of higher education. Now academic audit, redubbed 'quality audit', has been buttressed by the new procedure of quality assessment. Whereas audit takes the broader focus of a review of institutional mechanisms for quality assurance and is not directly linked to funding decisions, quality assessment focuses upon specific areas, and results in graded judgements of teaching quality which will in due course affect funding allocations. Universities deemed 'excellent' may be allocated an increase in fully-funded students – not a great prize, but nonetheless a significant one. Those whose teaching is judged 'unsatisfactory' will be formally warned and, if significant improvements do not follow, will be at risk of losing fully-funded students altogether.

This at least is the broad outline, but the approach to quality assessment being taken is still evolving – and evolving moreover in different ways in each of the three Funding Councils: HEFCE (Higher Education Funding Council for England), SHEFC (Scottish Higher Education Funding Council) and HEFCW (Higher Education Funding Council for Wales). These differences have been discussed in detail elsewhere (see, for example, Gordon and Partington 1993) but there are common elements to the approaches being taken which reflect criticisms arising from the pilot quality assessment visits.

Perhaps the most striking of these has been the incorporation of institutions' self-assessments of teaching quality within the subjects or 'cognate areas' concerned. The pilot assessments were vulnerable to criticism on the grounds of an over-reliance on the dubious practice of direct observation of teaching, and inadequate recognition of systematic internal checks on quality. There was thus a failure to acknowledge the progress made by most institutions in recent years in reviewing, strengthening and widening ownership of their internal quality control and assurance mechanisms (whether under the stimulus of academic audit, in the traditional universities; or of fresh thinking in the former polytechnics and colleges, following first accreditation and then university status; or of the broader influence of stiffer competition between institutions). Moreover, the approach initially followed for the pilot round seemed sadly out of touch with contemporary thinking on organizational change and indeed commercial and industrial practice on quality management. An essentially inspectorial approach combined with the distant prospect of public sanction was a very limited stratagem, it could be argued, if the real aim was to promote higher quality. It put institutions and their staff on the defensive; it secured change – where it could do so – by imposition rather than by consensus and wholehearted engagement; and it tended to foster a dependency relationship where responsibility for judgements about quality would be largely left to outside agencies rather than internally and widely shared and owned.

Happily, the Funding Councils have gone some way towards responding to these concerns. All three Funding Councils now place much greater emphasis on inviting and scrutinizing institutions' submissions, with the onus on the latter to suggest what grading might be most appropriate for a given subject area and to substantiate their judgement in their supporting documentation.

But what of the implications, for education development and the management of the curriculum, of this shift to accommodate a greater element of what might be called 'accountable self-review'? Clearly it is important to recognize that wider public as well as governmental concern for teaching quality – and for accountability for quality – is here to stay, and is more likely to wax rather than wane. This means that further sustained effort will be needed within universities to strengthen and support a quality commitment. Among the steps which might be considered are the following:

- More explicit publicizing of information about quality control and assurance methods in institutional publications, from course handbooks to prospectuses and annual reports.
- Similarly, greater efforts to disseminate information about examples of good practice and innovations in teaching, internally and externally (a vital step towards a more proactive approach to quality, breaking free of a passive and narrow reliance on performance indicators).
- Systematic briefing and training of all staff, whether in mainstream teaching or support roles, in quality control and assurance.
- Increased investment in helping staff to carry through quality-related procedures (e.g. in computerized processing of feedback on courses and teaching and in the provision of course-specific and student-specific performance information).

Nonetheless, there remain other issues which the universities themselves are not in a position to resolve. Accountability measures now take myriad (many would say a hotchpotch) forms: quality audit, quality assessment, accreditation visits by professional bodies, the external examining system, and of course universities' own internal procedures for monitoring and review. To these the Government has added, with ill-judged haste, 'Charters for Higher and Further Education' which set out the scope and level of information which institutions must provide to their students.

Besides leading to wasteful duplication of effort, there is, paradoxically, a serious threat to quality of teaching as the time and energies of large numbers of staff are diverted into meeting the requirements of these various competing procedures. Equally worryingly, no one has yet provided a satisfactory answer to the question of what will happen if two or more of these different procedures result in recommendations which are at odds with one another.

Sustaining and enhancing teaching quality

In this closing section, we consider specific strategies within universities for sustaining and, where feasible, enhancing the quality of teaching. Three strategies are reviewed:

- Recognizing and rewarding teaching excellence.
- Staff training and development.
- Seedcorn funding to promote good practice and innovation.

Recognition of teaching excellence

In the more traditional universities, the stimulus of academic audit in particular has teased out of the shadows the question of how far individual excellence in teaching is properly recognized and rewarded.

As interpreted in some universities, this means paying greater lip-service to teaching expertise in promotions to senior lecturer. But a less minimalist interpretation would argue that all universities will have to grapple with several other related issues. Not the least of these is the need to differentiate between competence and excellence in teaching, so that those with genuinely outstanding qualities as university teachers are distinguishable from those who are solidly competent and committed. This is not to belittle the value of teaching competence and commitment, both of which all universities need in large measures. But promotion on the grounds of teaching expertise should not be, as is sometimes the case, a consolation prize for long service or a reward for dogged enthusiasm for teaching in the face of colleagues' apathy. Excellent teachers have an impact that extends beyond their own day-to-day practice in one or more ways: an influence on their students that lasts long after they have ceased to teach them; an influence on departmental or faculty colleagues – whether by helping individuals to hone their teaching skills or by inspiring and carrying through changes to a range of courses or programmes of study; an influence nationally on curricular, teaching or assessment strategies in their discipline.

There is also the tricky question of how expertise in teaching, whether competent or excellent, can be satisfactorily documented. A practical way forward is being sought through the use of portfolios and profiles of teaching performance and achievements so that institutions will be unable to avoid paying serious attention to clarification of the criteria on which judgements of good practice are made. As a result, documentation of competence may well come to be seen as a requirement of all tenure and promotion candidates with teaching responsibilities, and not just sought from those giving priority to their teaching rather than to their research, development, consultancy, administrative or managerial performances.

Lastly, in taking steps towards more overt recognition of excellence in teaching, many universities have their sights rather narrowly set on the question of the senior or principal lectureship. Besides lamenting the unfortunate absence of a teaching title equivalent to that of 'Reader', we ought to be considering the award of Personal Chairs to teaching excellence as no less significant a benchmark of institutional commitment.

Staff training and development

As far as teaching is concerned, approaches to staff training and development have been undergoing a sea change in the last two or three years. The debate has moved on from the questions of whether or not staff development is a 'good thing' and where responsibility should be located to more pressing matters of substance. Three clear trends can be identified, all of which are likely to continue and intensify.

One such trend has been towards more overt attention to organizational as well as individual needs. Briefing and training programmes which were formerly geared in the main to the needs and aspirations of individual members of staff now tend to be much more strongly linked to policy developments and strategic initiatives, e.g. computer literacy, wider student access, quality assurance, course organization and the implications of larger classes, to take some Edinburgh examples. This is a much needed shift, since policymaking in universities generally has in the past often stopped short with the formal approval of a policy statement, rather than progressing to the less tractable questions of winning the consent of all staff, briefing them fully about changes under way, and assisting them in deploying the knowledge and skills needed to make that policy a reality. Using staff development programmes to address organizational needs of this kind is therefore a tool in the management of change which universities will find increasingly hard to do without.

Another and linked trend has been towards a network approach, where briefing and training programmes call on the expertise of a wide range of individuals within the institution with relevant expertise to be tapped. Compare this to past situations where a central unit has had to rely predominantly on the necessarily limited skills of its own staff, or where a lone staff development coordinator has had little option but to buy-in external trainers and workshop leaders who could only tailor their programmes to a restricted degree to local needs. The network approach holds out better prospects of realizing the ideal of a 'learning organization' which continually renews itself; it helps dissolve the boundaries between those who formulate policy, those who implement it and those on whom it impacts; and in the longer term it draws everyone into a net of informing, motivating, training and coaching others – an indispensable management skill.

The third trend has been to make programmes of initial training for university teachers a contractual requirement, often leading to a formal certificate or diploma. Indeed the Standing Conference on Educational Development has launched a pilot accreditation scheme which will give this further impetus (Baume 1992). But much more should be anticipated, particularly as attention has begun to switch beyond broad-brush induction into teaching. We shall see increased interest in preparation for restricted and ancillary teaching roles: contractually-linked training programmes for postgraduate tutors and laboratory demonstrators, as well as programmes for more experienced full-time staff taking up new responsibilities, whether as personal tutors, postgraduate research supervisors or external examiners. We should also be considering systematic training in the Cinderella skills of organizing and managing teaching – for organizers of course units and modules, directors of degree programmes, heads of departments, dean of faculties and those in the topmost managerial positions. (This will not be easily achieved, not least because of the pitifully small research and development effort which has so far gone into documenting and analysing what is required.) And lastly, we shall have to find better ways of tackling a pervasive difficulty – that resistant strain of more experienced staff who seem immune to any attempt to encourage them to review and update their teaching skills.

Seedcorn funding

Lastly, and briefly, it seems doubtful whether quality in teaching can be sustained in the longer term without the specific investment of resources in consolidating good practice and promoting innovation. One of the direct outcomes of the Enterprise in Higher Education programme has been to demonstrate to considerable benefits within institutions of making available relatively small sums of money for curriculum development and innovation – whether to pay for staff time, visits to other institutions or the production of learning materials. In a period when staff overload is commonplace, the impact of seedcorn funding of this kind is pivotal, and all universities will need to consider increasing the allocation of internal funds for this purpose as a form of capital investment in teaching quality.

Concluding comments

In this chapter, we have considered four interrelated facets of quality in teaching and what these might mean for curriculum management over the remainder of the decade. If there is a single theme that underlies these considerations, it is that curriculum and teaching questions, once seen in many universities as essentially localized concerns for course teams and departments, are now inescapably part of the mainstream of institutional decision-making and strategic planning, Equally significantly, sound management practice – whether in relation to teaching, research, consultancy or service to the community – is about much more than applying tools or devising structures and strategies. At base, it is concerned with goals and purposes and their relationship to process and outcomes.

In fact, hard thinking of this kind about teaching and learning seems inevitable, for the creation of a very much larger and more overtly university-based system of higher education, less obviously differentiated by institutional title, puts a bigger premium on institutional distinctiveness. (To use the jargon of marketing, each university must find its particular 'niche' within a complex and higher competitive marketplace.) At one level, self-evidently, this means striving for a particular balance between teaching, research development, and service to the local and regional community. But what will be the *specific* consequences of a given balance of activities for teaching, in terms of curriculum goals, teaching–learning processes and the attributes of graduates? What will be the distinctive stamp of teaching in, say, the research-orientated university, or the university which prides itself on its close links with employers, or the university which has made its mark by attracting a high proportion of Access and part-time students? Perhaps this is the starting-point for fundamental thinking in every university about the future management of the curriculum.

Notes

1. There is a dearth of literature on this topic. For a rare but not altogether convincing example, see Committee of Scottish Principals (1992: 77–86).
2. None of these possibilities needs be seen as mere conjecture: the first is already the case in subject areas such as Computer Science and Artificial Intelligence where there are abundant networked computing facilities, and wider opportunities will grow as campus-wide information systems become better established; the second has recently become a real possibility in subject areas such as Business and Management Studies; the third, fourth and fifth are to varying degrees represented in projects funded in summer 1992 under the UFC's Teaching and Learning Technology Programme; on the sixth, see Hounsell and Murray (1992); the seventh is already well established in several institutions including Oxford Brookes University and the Universities of Edinburgh and St Andrews.

References

Baume, C. (ed.) (1992) *SCED Teacher Accreditation Year Book*, Vol. 1. Standing Conference on Educational Development, Gala House, 3 Raglan Road, Edgbaston, Birmingham B5 7RA.

Bligh, D. (1972) *What's the Use of Lectures?*, 3rd edn. Penguin, Harmondsworth.

Boud, D. (1986) *Implementing Student Self-Assessment* (HERDSA Green Guides, No. 5). Higher Education Research and Development Society of Australasia, Kensington, NSW.

Brown, G. and Pendlebury, M. (1992) *Assessing Active Learning* (Effective Learning and Teaching in Higher Education, Module 11). CVCP Universities' Staff Development and Training Unit, Sheffield.

Committee of Scottish University Principals (1992) *Teaching and Learning in an Expanding Higher Education System.* Report of a Working Party of the Committee of Scottish University Principals, chaired by Professor A.G.J. MacFarlane. CSUP, Edinburgh.

Craft, A. (ed.) (1992) *Quality Assurance in Higher Education. Proceedings of an International Conference, Hong Kong, 1991.* Falmer Press, Brighton.

Cryer, P. and Elton, L. (1992) *Learning Actively on One's Own. Block B: Preparing Self-Instructional Materials* (Effective Learning and Teaching in Higher Education, Module 8). CVCP Universities' Staff Development and Training Unit, Sheffield.

Denicolo, P., Entwistle, N. and Hounsell, D. (1992) *What is Active Learning?* (Effective Learning and Teaching in Higher Education, Module 1). CVCP Universities' Staff Development and Training Unit, Sheffield.

Entwistle, N. (1992) *The Impact of Teaching on Learning Outcomes in Higher Education: A Literature Review.* CVCP Universities' Staff Development Unit/The Employment Department – Training, Enterprise and Education Directorate, Sheffield.

Entwistle, N. and Tait, H. (1992) *Learning Actively on One's Own. Block A: Promoting Effective Study Skills.* (Effective Learning and Teaching in Higher Education, Module 8). CVCP Universities' Staff Development and Training Unit, Sheffield.

Falchikov, N. and Boud, D. (1989) Student self-assessment in higher education: a meta-analysis. *Review of Educational Research,* 59(4), 395–430.

Gibbs, G. (n.d.) *Creating a Teaching Profile.* Technical and Educational Services, Bristol.

Gibbs, G. and Jenkins, A. (eds) (1992) *Teaching Large Classes in Higher Education: How to maintain quality with reduced resources.* Kogan Page, London.

Gordon, G. and Partington, P. (1993) *Quality in Higher Education: overview and update* (USDU Briefing Paper 3). CVCP Universities' Staff Development Unit, Sheffield.

Griffiths, S. and Partington, P. (1992) *Enabling Active Learning in Small Groups* (Effective Learning and Teaching in Higher Education, Module 5). CVCP Universities' Staff Development and Training Unit, Sheffield.

Hartley, J. and Bahra, H. (1992) Study networks: support mechanisms for large groups of part-time students, in Gibbs, G. and Jenkins, A. (eds) *Teaching Large Classes in Higher Education: how to maintain quality with reduced resources.* pp. 130–7. Kogan Page, London.

Hounsell, D. and Murray, R. (1992) *Essay Writing for Active Learning* (Effective Learning and Teaching in Higher Education, Module 9). CVCP Universities' Staff Development and Training Unit, Sheffield.

Jacques, D. (1984) *Learning in Groups.* Croom Helm, London.

Rowntree, D. (1990) *Teaching Through Self Instruction* (rev. edn). Kogan Page, London.

Seldin, P. (1991) *The Teaching Portfolio.* Anker, Bolton, Mass.

7

A Course Leader's Perspective

Mary N. Haslum

The challenge implicit in the University's mission is that of reconciling growth, student choice, and wider access, whilst maintaining the quality of existing provision.[1]

The four themes of wider access, student choice, growth and quality of provision guide my discussion of a Course Leader's perspective of developments in the Higher Education (HE) curriculum. My perspective is influenced inevitably by the particular HE institution in which I am working but I try to draw out points from this which contribute to a general discussion on managing change in the curriculum.

My thesis is that many of the implementation costs of the changes in the HE curriculum are, and will continue to be, hidden as they fall not on senior management but on the people who drive the system and deliver the courses.

In the past, I have been a Course Leader for a small part-time diploma course in research methods supporting about 15 mature health-care students to become researchers within their own professions. Now I am a Course Leader of a new honours degree with an intake of 90 full-time and 10 part-time students a year. It is an award route in a modular programme and some of its modules are offered in an evening programme for a part-time Combined Studies degree. In company with colleagues in many HE institutions, the pressure is on to change, to change quickly and to change effectively. For many of us this means inventing the wheel as we are using it.

Wider access

In the 1992 Bolland Lecture at Bristol Polytechnic, Peter Scott argued that 'Mass or, at any rate, much wider access is the key phenomenon in shaping the new higher education, organizationally and intellectually.'[2] It has been stated more cynically by Smith and Saunders: 'So access is important not because of a commitment to ideals of education or civilized humanity but because the economy requires more graduates and higher education must be responsive to their production.'[3]

Greater access means that courses will take not just more students but more students with a greater variety of interests, backgrounds, skills and entrance qualifications.[4–6] Scott and Watson noted in Chapter 1 that non-standard entrants now make up one-third of new entrants. As the deliverers of courses we need to know about this increasing diversity in order to plan for it more effectively and to ensure that new applicants are treated equitably.

The proportion of women students is also increasing.[6,7] Many women entering HE, however, already have full-time jobs as housekeepers and mothers. These do not cease when they become students. If HE institutions are serious about wider access they must tackle the growing need for low-cost day care and crèche facilities.

Mature students (over 21 years old) tend not to have standard entry qualifications but Bourner and Hamed[8] found that they fared at least as well as standard entrants on degree and diploma courses. Currently, 1 in 6 people in England is over 65 years of age. By the year 2020, this will have increased to 1 in 4. Many people are 'retiring' (or being made redundant) long before age 65. Hopson and Scally[9] have argued for over a decade now that Lifeskills training is lifelong, and continuing education will have to allow for the inclusion of many more people from the older age groups in the years to come.

Greater access should mean greater access for students with disabilities. Provision for such students is a continuing source of debate and dissatisfaction in HE institutions. The Open University is at the forefront of support with a policy of positive discrimination which guarantees admission. There have been several OU initiatives on communication via home computing for students with hearing and vision impairments.[10] In spite of this, the OU still stresses that for most students with disabilities, and particularly young students, conventional HE institutions may offer a more appropriate educational experience because of the social and learning contacts they tend to foster.[11]

If HE institutions are where students with disabilities should be, and where they will come as access increases, to what extent are HE institutions able to support them and prepared not to discriminate against them? The NAFTHE survey, announced recently, will attempt to identify good practice and spot gaps in provision. Areas covered will include: the recruitment of students; curriculum resources; harassment; staff development; monitoring; and health and safety issues.[12]

There is still relatively little data on the participation of ethnic minorities in post-compulsory and higher education. Thirty-four per cent are currently under the age of 15 years compared with 20 per cent of white people. This suggests a greater potential participation in HE in the future. The 1987 Labour Market Survey showed similar proportions of white and ethnic minority people have degree-level qualifications (6 per cent) but many of the qualifications of the latter were probably obtained outside the UK.[13] Data on people from ethnic minorities entering HE should improve with the inclusion of ethnic monitoring by UCAS.

Students from overseas, in contrast to students from indigenous ethnic minorities, come with a different set of expectations. Kimmell[14] has argued that HE institutions have seen them primarily as a means of increasing revenue but that overseas students now see themselves as clients prepared to pay for a high-quality service. The onus is on us to provide the type and amount of support they need and for this, staff development and training is urgently needed.

Reforms in secondary education over the last decade have also served to increase the heterogeneity of the student population. Even amongst the traditional A Level qualifications there are developments. In 1989, the half A Level (AS Level) was introduced. A Levels are now offered in subjects not previously taught outside HE but what does one do with these students? There is a reluctance to grant them 'Advanced Standing' and exemptions when they have covered in breadth what the first-year undergraduates will cover in depth.

Although A Levels do not predict final degree categories very well we hope high grades identify students who are able to interact effectively in tutorials and seminars, plan written work, write clearly and grammatically, punctuate, spell, read for understanding and who have begun to think analytically and creatively for themselves. GCSE and the National Curriculum are currently affecting the way secondary-school pupils are taught. Hopefully such changes will improve the development of these 'core skills'.

The General National Vocational Qualification (GNVQ) and NVQ was announced as the mainstream national provision for vocational education and training in a White Paper in 1991.[15] One of the main objectives is to provide an alternative to A Levels (GNVQ Level 3). Level 4 will equate with degree-level work.

There is little doubt that consideration of training outcomes was long overdue but the new system is not without its critics. Hodgkinson[16] suggested that the NVQs are ill-equipped to meet the needs of students on full-time vocational courses and may not contribute significantly to student empowerment because of employer control of the system. Marshall[17] has argued that the functionalist and behaviourist approach on which the assessment is based has led to rigid performance criteria. There is little room for individuality or any constructive contribution from the trainee. Ashworth[18] goes further, drawing a distinction between 'having NCVQ competencies' and 'being competent'. Without further development, it appears that these qualifications are unlikely to reassure admissions tutors of the suitability of applicants.

Between 1982 and 1987, the numbers of students on BTEC courses increased by 50 per cent. About 10,000 of the 30,000 who gain relevant BTECs move on to study a first degree.[6] Redpath and Harvey[19] have suggested that people with BTEC qualifications are more likely to have taken them for vocational and career reasons than to gain access to HE. The BTEC students on my course are coping well.

Widening access has a direct knock-on effect on the already hugely expensive admissions process. People enter or return to formal education for many reasons; often to seek better job qualifications, to fulfil a personal need or just for something different to do. Whilst Local Education Authority and Education Guidance Services and TAPs (Training Access Points), Citizens' Advice Bureaux and Job Centres provide a lot of information, educational institutions are seen as the most appropriate source of information and guidance.[20] But at what point should educational advice be given?

This year on my course, the majority of queries came from adults, either parents of 18-year-olds or mature applicants. Often, the admissions procedure begins with a telephone enquiry (5–20 minutes of staff time) followed by other calls or letters (which have to be answered). We try to persuade applicants, and it is usually mature applicants, to read the UCAS handbook and the information they have been sent, but they would much rather talk to us. We invite some of them for interview but it is a high-cost activity. Some come for a visit uninvited. If we offer them a place they ring up for more information on the course and want to talk to the course adviser about first year options; if we turn them down, they want to know why; then they ring up and want to be reconsidered. The processing of applicants is a staff-expensive activity which will mushroom with the increase of people coming from non-traditional routes, particularly as each needs and demands more care.

The extent to which the admissions process is handled by a central unit varies between institutions. What is clear is that the demand for information and guidance is increasing dramatically. If HE institutions are serious about widening access, the responsibility for guidance and Accreditation of Prior Experience and Learning (APEL) has to be shouldered clearly and unequivocally. It probably does not matter whether this is provided by independent units in HE institutions or in partnership with Educational Guidance Services. It is a labour-intensive service and it is too high a cost to be borne by course teams.

Student choice: modularization

Another element in managing the HE curriculum is the development of student choice and flexibility of mode of study. The vehicle by which some institutions have chosen to develop this is modularization. Since the last 18 months of my life have been spent modularizing, and helping others to modularize, I am going to pursue my theme of the human cost involved in changing the HE curriculum within the context of modularization.

A module is a free-standing unit of study with defined student study hours. Choice increases as the menu of modules is developed. Modules can be delivered during the day, evening, weekend or at summer school. They can last a whole year or a few weeks. A user-friendly timetable for study is offered for full- and part-time students and the distinction between them all but disappears. Modules are discrete units of study which are assessed on completion of the work defined for them and 'credits' are awarded on the basis of successful completion. Modularization together with the Credit Accumulation and Transfer Scheme (CATS) enables the user not only to choose the time of day to study but also the time of life. Sixty credits gained at Level 1 three years ago may now be increased by the study of more modules.

In the 1970s, modularization was seen as a means of overcoming artificial subject boundaries, promoting student choice and clarifying course objectives, but Squires[21] has argued that interest in it now appears to come from a desire for administrative rationalization and the promotion of credit transfers between courses, institutions and modes of delivery.

There appear to be two main models for going modular. One is the creation model whereby the old is replaced by a new modular version 'overnight'; the other is the incremental model where it happens more gradually with more control given to the people who do the changing. My own institution adopted an incremental model inviting individual faculties to develop their own modular programmes within a fairly generous timescale. There does not, however, appear to be a painless way of going modular. This is probably more to do with the way people adapt to change than anything inherently awful in modularization. We used the incremental model in my faculty which, with hindsight, was a mistake. It would have been easier if we had spent much more time planning, developing systems, briefing staff and then gone modular overnight.

A major advantage of modularization is that it invites, if not demands, a review of the curriculum. Some courses try to avoid this by just doing a little repackaging, drawing boxes around already existing units of study and calling them modules. This is 'linear modularization' and does not allow for student choice. Others insert some options in an otherwise linear model, whilst still others genuinely offer alternative pathways of modules for students to follow to a named award.

The question of choice is a particular problem for courses involving a professional qualification where the curriculum is often defined by an external body. The day when most undergraduates in Nursing, Physiotherapy or Radiography, for example, are offered and take the opportunity to study Geography, German or Geophysics, is still a long way off. The problem is that these courses have considerable mandatory practice hours and there is little time to study anything not directly related to clinical training. In any case, you may prefer to be nursed by someone who has successfully completed a module on infection control rather than Modern Art or Mediæval History, although this may depend on what is wrong with you. Post-registration degrees could permit greater choice but for this to happen the new 'top-up' degrees have to be located in wider modular programmes.

Flexibility is seen as an important principle in providing for part-time students in HE but, although the length of time for a diploma or degree may be flexible, the students' demands can impose limitations on the time-table. Students from the health-care professions and industry tend to study on a day-release basis. Modules for a particular level of the part-time nursing degree route, for example, therefore have to run in a single day.

Part-time degrees usually have a limit of nine years for completion but some professional degree courses must have a shorter 'shelf-life' to ensure that graduates are up to date in theory and professional practice.

Flexibility and student choice are both constrained by institutional limitations. Lack of appropriately-sized teaching rooms and laboratories leads to 'timetabling problems'. Trying to fit particular sized groups of students in rooms with staff to teach them is a major source of frustration anyway but seems to be much worse in a modular programme. Oxford Brookes University solves it by allocating a module to a timetable slot as a first priority and then coping with the rest of the problems.[22] Course Leaders on traditional courses, however, are used to constructing their own timetables and negotiating servicing from there. Consequently, trying to work out how to run non-modular and modular courses in the same department provides painful lessons on the limitations of the human mind.

We have viewed and test-driven automatic timetabling software but a lot of energy is needed to learn how to use them and whilst they cope with timetabling with impressive speed and efficiency, they only sort out the logic not the problem. Messages such as 'No room available to take group size specified' or 'Module cannot run at time stated' will provide the last straws for many a well-intentioned member of staff in the years to come.

When courses were courses, Course Leaders knew who their students were, planned when they came in, what they did, when they did it, who taught them and kept a parental eye on them as well. But courses are not courses any more – they are award routes made up of a variety of modules. Whilst students may benefit from studying alongside peers with different interests, module leaders need to know how many should be in the room, who they are and to which award route they belong. The need to link admission, registration and module management information systems is paramount. In a perfect HE institution, all students would enrol on time, module quotas would be neither under- nor over-subscribed, timetabling would run like clockwork, assessment results would be handled with speed and efficiency and whizz round field examining boards and award and progression boards without a hitch. Do you work in such an institution?

Managements in HE institutions have to balance the promotion of educational vision and the potential for change against resource implications. I do not believe, however, that the human cost of going modular is fully appreciated. The rethinking of course content which modularization engenders is hugely expensive of staff time and energy. The redeveloping of 'course' administration and its accompanying information system requires immense mental and emotional effort by many people. Some of the development costs are unforeseeable and unintended, and probably incalculable.

The staff experience of HE changes

I made the assertion at the beginning that we have been inventing the wheel at the same time as using it. This is partly the penalty of following an incremental model. Oxford Brookes University has been modularizing for over two decades and still is not fully modular. We have modularized from the bottom up and probably had the worst of all worlds by pursuing a creation model in a non-creationist faculty. Although it might have been seen as undermining the autonomy of academic staff, it might have been easier if the faculty, if not the institution, had modularized 'overnight' and the change had been driven from the top down.

We semesterized our modules as well. With hindsight, I cannot see why. Doubling up the examining boards (now at the end of each 15-week semester) makes twice the work and how does a week off in the middle of February (intersemester week) help anyone? If modules have to have standard time packaging why not have 5-, 10-, 15-, 30-week modules and all the examination boards at the end of the academic year?

We have invented everything from the modules, their delivery and assessments, to the programme timetable and the principles of the information systems. We have defined responsibilities for Field Leaders, Module Leaders, Award Route Leaders and thought up the composition of umpteen committees, devised the lines of information flow and accountability. We have designed module evaluation sheets, module exemption forms and APEL statements. The biggest lesson we learned was to stop waiting for someone out there to decide what to do and to decide for ourselves. One of the penalties of going in the water first is that other people, faculties, institutions want you to advise them how not to make the mistakes you made. This can be very time consuming.

We have learned some interesting lessons this year. It is quite easy to lose a student in a modular programme, particularly at the beginning of the year. Students take modules across a number of fields, even programmes, and some of the modules have many students. Since they are not required to report in and are not electronically tagged it can be days before one is missed. We do have a personal tutor/student adviser system but you cannot make them come to see you. Next year, the main aim of the student induction programme will be to help students develop their own support networks.

The assessment timetable can be a nightmare for students and staff. Many modules are assessed on coursework. It is very difficult to devise hand-in dates to give a reasonable spread across the year, especially when some of the modules are laboratory based. If it is difficult between modules in the same field it is almost impossible between fields.

Finding time to give feedback to so many students on coursework is difficult. We have developed a standardized assessment sheet which is given in with the work to be marked. A student can specify any area in which feedback is particularly required. It also helps students to understand the basis on which the work is assessed.

I think we have to develop a model of educational delivery which is team-based and supported by modern technology just as a medical or surgical consultant has a team of medical or surgical assistants, theatre and ward staff, hi-tech equipment and a hospital administration information system. If you do not expect me to mend the video-playback machine why do I have to spend time in front of a photocopier? Why does the switchboard put all the course enquiries through to me? I could have a secretary, administrator and, most important a clerical assistant, allocated to my Field or Award Route. A member of the library staff could work with us to develop library resources for the modules. If I had a networked PC on my desk, I could send my handouts to the network laser printer, access the library index and lending system to put books on short loan at assignment writing times, interrogate the library CD-ROMs for my research and to support the scholarly work I do not have time to do, send messages round the campus, even the world. Maybe I could engage in computer conferencing and hold tutorials by telephone link.[23]

Colleagues in modular institutions will be aware of students' apparent need for a course identity. Who are your fellow travellers? What do they think of the experience you are all having? The Award Route Leader is responsible for the students' experience of the Route and chairs the Award Route Management Committee which has student representatives. We have encouraged the students to develop their own Route-based society. I am not sure whether Award Route identity should be positively promoted in a modular programme or left to see if it will be replaced by something wider and more outward looking.

For many staff, the increase in student numbers means teaching larger and larger groups in bigger and bigger lecture theatres. The exercise becomes one of voice projection and crowd control. Interaction with the audience is difficult because even if they hear what you say, you will not hear what they reply or ask. HE institutions cannot afford to build numerous large lecture theatres. The increase in students will have to be accommodated within the existing plant. Having said that, if more existing teaching rooms were equipped with good audio-visual presentation systems and air conditioning, the HE experience for both students and staff would be greatly enhanced.

One consequence of the impersonal delivery of lectures to large groups is that many students, particularly mature students, seek help from staff on a one-to-one basis outside formal teaching time; but, non-allocated time spent sorting you out means less time to do the rest of my work. Whilst staff have to learn to say 'No' and adopt better ways of coping by running surgeries and appointments systems, a fundamental change is needed in the way staff and students view the educational process.

A possible key to improving cost effectiveness of course delivery, appears to lie in promoting Independent Student Learning (ISL). This could be construed as a euphemism for 'increasing the staff:student ratio' but it does have a sound educational basis. Whilst modularization increases student choice and flexibility of study, and may also have the effect of revitalizing content, ISL strikes at the heart of the educational process itself and could be used not just to 'maintain the quality of provision' but rather to improve the quality of student learning.

Research by the Centre for Higher Education Studies[24] shows what we knew in our hearts already, that the primary issue identified by students as enabling effective teaching and learning is the motivation and personality of their teachers. Enthusiastic, interested, charismatic teachers with good presentation skills are valued above all else. Most academic staff realize that there are few more rewarding experiences in education than when a student understands what is being said and moves past and beyond, seeing new horizons and catching the excitement of the quest for understanding. The 'nurturing until you can stand on your own' approach is rewarding for both staff and students but costly of staff time and not necessarily the only, nor the most appropriate, way to promote independent student learning or improve the quality of learning.

Improving the quality of student learning

What have you done in the last year to improve the quality of learning for your students? What do you mean by quality of learning? People have different perceptions of quality and different criteria. The strategy used to improve quality of learning will contain an implicit value orientation. Institutional cost probably figures strongly in management criteria whilst personal cost is likely to be significant, amongst others, for academic staff.

The CNAA recently sponsored a project on improving student learning which defined quality in educational terms. The general aim was:

> the development of students' intellectual and imaginative powers; their understanding and judgment; their ability to communicate; their ability to see relationships within what they have learned and to perceive this field of study in a broader perspective ... to stimulate an enquiring, analytical and creative approach, encouraging independent judgment and critical self-awareness.[25]

Who could ask for anything more? But in 1989, the HMI commentary 'The English Polytechnics' noted

> an over-dependence on one way of teaching – often the formal lecture – so that students do not develop a range of skills appropriate to higher education; spoon feeding in lectures, seminars and practical work, so that students become over-dependent on the information selected and provided for them by their teachers; assessment methods which place too high a premium on the ability to recall factual information.[26]

Many of the courses we deliver have too great an emphasis on memorizing information and too little on trying to understand and apply the knowledge. This can be exacerbated by assessment procedures which require students to memorize facts, what Marton and Saljo[27,28] call 'surface learning', rather than challenge them to make sense of what is presented (the 'deep approach' to learning).

A surface learning approach is very common and found on most courses to a greater or lesser extent. Ramsden[29] reported it was common in all subject areas in HE and more common in universities than polytechnics. There are wide differences in the patterns of learning which courses promote within institutions as well as between them.[30]

It is interesting to ask whether there are stable individual differences in approaches to learning. The Oxford study[25] suggested that whilst differences are extremely wide, they can also be highly volatile. Given the opportunity, students could switch dramatically, within a few weeks, from an extreme surface approach to an extreme deep approach to learning. Many students can switch between the two approaches depending on the demands a course makes upon them.

The important conclusion of the study was that it is possible to change students' approach to learning and thereby improve the quality of their learning. Gibbs[25] emphasizes the importance of helping students to develop intrinsic motivation which comes from an interest in the subject and a desire to understand, rather than extrinsic motivation which comes from outside influences such as assessment demands. His message is that the appropriate focus for changing the approach to learning is course design and process rather than teaching and content.

Others have made similar arguments; Schon,[31] for example, asserts that professional education should be centred on enhancing a practitioner's ability for 'reflection-in-action', that is, learning by doing and developing the ability for continued learning and problem solving throughout the professional's career.

Promoting independent student learning and improving the quality of learning involves for most of us a rethinking of ideas on the educational process and our roles within it. Just as modularization involves enormous staff effort in rethinking fundamental issues, so does this. Even if we take some courses 'off the shelf' they probably will still have to be tailored to fit. Effects of the changes in course design must be monitored and evaluated. We will find ourselves engaged in educational action research on a large scale. Like modularization, the development costs are enormous.

Conclusion

Going modular has changed my job and those of my colleagues dramatically and it is probably too soon to make anything other than an interim judgement of the experience. The task facing the university was how to transfer a very heavily course-dominated institution to a more flexible modular structure with much greater potential for educational development. This was bound to be difficult and perhaps at faculty or programme level it is easy to be unaware of the extent of management activity and support that is provided. Certainly where it has been overt, for example, in the setting up of a university modular steering group, or in the informal Field and Award Route Leaders' committee it has been much appreciated. In both these examples it was possible to experience management operating as a two-way process and it felt good.

There have been considerable changes in the infrastructure of many HE institutions associated mainly with the shift from 'management' to 'strategic' cultures (Chapter 2) but also associated with modularization. Generally, this has involved considerable adaptation to changes in roles and working practices for many administrative and academic staff.

New pressures continue to appear. The re-emphasis of scholarly activity and its contribution to the research assessment exercise is for many in the newer universities particularly hard; not because of an unwillingness to take part but an inability to reduce workloads sufficiently to permit participation. Even changing lecture-based modules to distance learning units involves huge start-up costs.

Matching curriculum organization to a more diverse entry group is a difficult and complex problem. Moreover, the relationship between teachers and students is changing. Encouraged by multi-mode attendance, module choice, endless requests for module evaluations and our own determination that they should see us as partners in their learning, students treat us more and more as indefatigable providers of a continually available service. A growing number of mature and 'streetwise' students expect a combined academic and personal counselling service (the two are inseparable in their minds) on demand.

We have to reduce the labour-intensive activities in course delivery. Marking 200 essays, for example, is a different experience from marking twenty. We have to find a way of providing constructive feedback to many more students which takes less of our time. We could return to examinations; make much more use of computer-marked assignments; persuade students to mark each other's work. At the University of Nottingham, Richard Gentle has developed THESYS, a computer-aided assessment guide for third-year research projects, for students and staff. For those activities that cannot be reduced, we must develop the teaching support teams discussed earlier.

The challenge of the recent changes in HE has had its moments and I remain committed to the vision which fired it. The changes will continue because rethinking course design along the lines discussed makes sound educational sense. The changes ahead seem greater than the changes behind, and I find myself wanting to re-emphasize the advice offered by Black and Sparks[32] about ten years ago:

Innovations in teaching need particular support and protection if they are to develop to their full potential and if the staff involved are to have a fair reward for the risks they take.

Notes

1. Morris, A. *Bristol's New University: Summary of Strategic Guidelines 1992–6.* University of the West of England.
2. Scott, P. (1992) *Mass Higher Education: towards a new learning economy.* Bolland Lecture, Bristol Polytechnic.
3. Smith, D.M. and Saunders, M.R. (1991) *Other Routes: Part-time Higher Education Policy.* The Society for Research into Higher Education and Open University Press, Buckingham.
4. Statistical Report. *Training Skills Bulletin 1988.*
5. Department of Education and Science (1988) Mature Students in Higher Education. *Statistical Bulletin,* 11.
6. Pearson, R., Pike, G., Gordon, A., Weyman, C. (1989) *How Many Graduates in the 21st Century? – The Choice is Yours.* Institute of Manpower Studies Report No. 177.
7. Smithers, A. and Robinson, P. (1989) *Increasing Participation in Higher Education.* University of Manchester Press.
8. Bourner, T. and Hamed, M. (1987) *Entry Qualification and Degree Performance,* 10. CNAA Development Services, London.
9. Hopson, B. and Scally, H. (1981) *Lifeskills Teaching.* McGraw-Hill, Maidenhead.
10. Vincent, T. *et al.* (1988) Disabled students, computers and distance teaching. Some experiences from the Open University, and implications. *Media in Education and Development,* 21(4), 157–62.
11. *Skill: A Guide to Higher Education for People with Disabilities* (1990) National Bureau for Students with Disabilities, London.
12. NATFHE to launch disability survey. *NATFHE Journal* (1992), 2, 24.
13. *The Labour Market for New Graduates 1987. Department of Education and Science Economic Bulletin* (1989), No. 1.
14. Kimmell, M. (1990) *The Learning Experiences of Overseas Students.* The Society for Research into Higher Education and the Open University Press, Buckingham.
15. HMSO. *Education and Training in the Twenty First Century,* May 1991, London.
16. Hodginkson, P. (1991) NCVQ and the 16–19 Curriculum. *British Journal of Education and Work,* 4, 3.
17. Marshall, K. (1991) NVQs as assessment of 'Outcomes'. *Journal of Further and Higher Education,* 15, 3.
18. Ashworth, P. (1992) Being competent and having 'competencies'. *Journal of Further and Higher Education,* 16, 3.
19. Redpath, B. and Harvey, B. (1987) *Young People's Intentions to Enter Higher Education.* OPCS/HMSO, London.
20. *The Challenge of Change* (1987) Unit for the Development of Adult and Continuing Education.
21. Squires, G. (1990) *First Degree: the undergraduate curriculum.* Society for Research into Higher Education and the Open University Press. Buckingham.
22. Watson, D. (1989) *Managing the Modular Course: Perspectives from Oxford Polytechnic.* The Society for Research into Higher Education and Open University Press, Buckingham.

23. Mason, R. (1989) *The Use of Computer Networks in Education and Training. Report to the Training Agency.* Open University, Buckingham.
24. Centre for Higher Education Studies (1992) Identifying and developing a quality ethos for teaching in higher education. *CHES Newsletter,* February, No. 2.
25. Gibbs, G. (1992) *Improving the Quality of Student Learning.* Technical and Educational Services Ltd, Bristol.
26. HMI (1989) *The English Polytechnics.* HMSO, London.
27. Marton, F. and Saljo, R. (1976) On qualitative differences in learning – 1: outcome and process. *British Journal of Educational Psychology,* 46, 4–11.
28. Marton, F. and Saljo, R. (1984) Approaches to Learning. In Marton, F., Hounsell, D. and Enwhistle, N.J. (eds) *The Experience of Learning.* Scottish Academic Press, Edinburgh.
29. Ramsden, P. (1992) Lost in the crowd? *Higher Education,* July 17, 15.
30. Ramsden, P. (1983) Institutional variations in British students' approaches to learning and experience of teaching. *Higher Education,* 12, 691–705.
31. Schon, D.A. (1988) *Educating the Reflective Practitioner.* Jossey-Bass, San Francisco.
32. Black, P. and Sparks, S.J. (1982) Teaching and learning. In Bligh, D. (ed.) *Professionalism and Flexibility in Learning. Research into Higher Education Monograph.* Society for Research into Higher Education, Guildford.

8

Curriculum Change and Professional Identity: The Role of the University Lecturer

Jean Bocock

To begin with an anecdote: a group of newly recruited academic staff recently assembled for a seminar as part of a programme of pedagogic training and support offered by their employing university. In earlier sessions the values they brought to their teaching had been identified and this had guided a discussion about approaches to teaching and learning. On this occasion they were joined by the Vice-Chancellor who talked to them about institutional mission and objectives and staff contribution to their realization. The staff in turn shared with him their earlier discussions concerning professional educational values. The Vice-Chancellor listened, nodded sympathetically, and then said, 'But you see we cannot afford your values!'

This story sums up the dilemma facing many institutions, their managers and staff. How do universities and colleges which have hitherto offered to academic staff high levels of autonomy in teaching and research, now cope with a situation in which the professional values many of those staff espouse can no longer be 'afforded'? There is a remarkable degree of consensus in these chapters both about the extent of changes which have already occurred and the scale of change now required if there is to be a further shift towards the more open access system required by Government participation targets. Scott and Watson in Chapters 1 and 2 describe many of these changes and their consequences; King in Chapter 4 suggests more fundamental change is required. Hitherto, he asserts, the impact of managerial initiatives has been on the way the curriculum is organized, packaged and delivered. This has caused problem enough. He suggests, however, that there is a need for greater managerial control over the product (i.e. curriculum itself) and that the challenge of wider access will not only break the monopoly which academic staff enjoy over curriculum styles and delivery, but also attenuate their control over its content. If this prediction is accurate, it is likely that the ongoing debate concerning the rights, opportunities and obligations of academics to undertake research will be overtaken and engulfed by a much more fundamental debate about the roles and responsibilities of lecturers.

Let me be clear. I do not in any way suggest that what Professor King proposes is an old-fashioned attack on academic freedom. I also think he is right that there is likely to be 'more extensive corporate curiosity' – to use his phraseology – in the curriculum than hitherto. He is equally right in his assessment that this poses as many problems and challenges for management styles and structures as it does for lecturers and other staff. For whereas once most higher education managers would have been equally legitimated as academics, and therefore able to switch roles and functions effectively, the greater degree of executive managerialism, particularly prevalent in the new universities has rendered that path a non-starter for many.

What then does this imply for the role of university lecturers? Greater diversity of intake and institutional mission must surely imply increasing diversity of role for academics. Although there may have been greater consensus in the past, when a smaller more unitary system of higher education transforms itself, then greater diversity is bound to prevail. This will not simply be a further extension of the old divisions between those passionately committed to research leaving others to derive greater professional satisfaction from teaching. Rather the consequence of educational and curriculum change is highlighting the need for many kinds of teaching and learning support which would not hitherto have formed part of the university curriculum. Such change also brings in its wake a potential broadening of the profession as new categories of academic (support) staff increasingly interface with the curriculum and its delivery.

At a simple level these changes are reflected in several programmes – Mathematics and Engineering come readily to mind – where the assumed 'starting point' of many courses can no longer be taken for granted with the greater diversity of student entry. Programmes are therefore devised to remedy the identified deficiencies. Many universities now also offer programmes across the curriculum – languages and information technology skills for example. Since 'traditional' university lecturers (by that I here mean those who are interested in language and information technology as more than an instrumental skill) are not always pedagogically equipped to undertake such teaching, others may be employed. A number of the projects supported under the HEFCE's (Higher Education Funding Council for England) Teaching and Learning Technology Programme are devising learning packages which can be delivered by 'non-specialists'; they too are particularly targeted at early years of degree courses.[1]

Many of these examples are part of the wider trend to make much of undergraduate teaching less specialist. Many universities are now recognizing that the greater diversity of entrants to higher education, combined with increasing demands from employers for evidence of core-transferable skills, requires that at least the initial phase of higher education should provide a broad general grounding in key skills and competences. Even those who reject King's notion of 'core/foundation curricula' acknowledge that the increasing spread of modular and credit-based systems is leading at a minimum to deferred undergraduate specialization and in their more radical form to undergraduate degrees which are not solely or even primarily defined by established disciplinary boundaries.

The key changes

In discussing the challenges which credit-based systems pose to traditional academic practices, values and patterns of institutional organization, Scott has identified four paradigm shifts.[2] Using the same analytical framework it is possible to identify the implications of such shifts for the role of the lecturer.

Courses to credits

Most existing lecturers in the system are themselves the product of a three or four years honours degree, probably single-subject or joint Honours. Such courses predominate in the traditional university sector and indeed still remain the central pattern in many institutions. They not only reflect a particular organizational pattern but also academic assumptions and values particularly about the organization of knowledge. Most academics were initiated into particular disciplinary and/or professional frameworks which in turn they seek to transmit to the next generation of students. In contrast to these disciplinary and professional cultures, credit systems offer students wider entry into a much more diffuse culture of higher education. Lecturers are no longer 'in charge' since they cannot so readily predetermine the path which students will follow.

Courses, particularly those organized around specific disciplines, have also provided both staff and students with identities and therefore perhaps a sense of community, e.g. as historians, engineers or lawyers. Such communities can, in the ideal world, also be learning communities reinforcing informally the organizational patterns of lectures and seminars. This is an important aspect of the academic intimacy to which Scott and Watson refer in Chapter 2. As Robertson, himself a key proponent of CATS acknowledges:

> There is the suspicion that proposed changes will negatively affect, not just material conditions, but the intellectual and cultural integrity of professional life itself. The power of the adherence to subject and disciplinary culture, particularly within higher education, has been

elegantly documented (Becher 1989) and reinforced by the recognition that the organizational arrangements of institutional life also impede radical change (Becher and Kogan 1992).[3]

In the past everyone knew where they were; disciplines and courses had clear and delineated boundaries. Recent developments in the organization and delivery of learning are weakening boundaries, and with them the sense of identity which staff, in particular, have built up and around which they have organized their professional lives over so many years. This loss of professional identity is not easily reconstituted in credit-based systems where disciplinary expertise alone, hitherto the foundation stone of academic reputation, is often seen to be insufficient in itself. More is now being demanded of lecturers.

Departments to frameworks

This loss can easily be reinforced by the second shift, from subject departments to much looser academic frameworks, which often accompanies the introduction of credit systems and modular courses. One of the 'guest leaders' in *The Times Higher Education Supplement* noted:

> In a modularised environment, doing a degree is not a matter of initiation into a well-defined intellectual and social space, but is a series of encounters with an increasingly wide range of discourses, techniques and people. The administrative groupings needed to give students a home base . . . may still be tied to subject disciplines or intellectual areas, but cannot have the circumscribing effects on students' outlooks which tend to be exercised by traditional departments.[4]

Even in institutions less substantially affected by credit and modular systems, the same process can be seen at work. In the recent assessment report on history at the University of Leicester the 'separate nature of the two (i.e. history) departments' was noted and the assessors 'urge consideration of the creation of a School of Historical Studies at Leicester and feel the move to modularisation might spur this on . . .'[5]

Credit systems inevitably provide for greater central control of the organization of the curriculum and in this way become part of the shifting balance of power in institutions in which lecturers often define themselves as being on the 'losing' side. Greater control over resource allocation is, of course, now frequently devolved to cost centres but they in turn are simultaneously deprived of much of their old autonomy (as academic departments) to shape academic programmes. From predominantly academic entities they are being transformed into management units in which management skills are seen to be equally as important as academic skills particularly for professors/middle managers. This too can reinforce the sense of academic devaluation experienced by many lecturers.

Subject-based teaching to student-centred learning

The spread of credit systems and modular courses also places increasing control of the learning process in the hands of students.

> The new culture of learning is likely to depart sharply from arrangements which rely exclusively upon professional academic definitions of appropriate learning needs, upon closely marshalled patterns of student choice, or upon the vested interests of institutions. Instead, it is likely that students-as-learners will be invited to exercise substantially greater control over definitions of personal learning needs, less constrained by the historic judgements of their academic tutors.[6]

Students, in turn, seek guidance not only from lecturers but also from learning support staff including those involved in educational guidance and counselling. This shift may also be perceived as devaluing the role of the lecturer, who is redefined as a facilitator of the learning process rather than an expert in a particular disciplinary area. Not only is the knowledge base of lecturers apparently undervalued but many academics also feel they lack the skills required of them in the new forms of higher education. They are being asked to redefine their roles but frequently given inadequate support and assistance in doing so.

One academic wrote recently to *The Guardian*:

> I am not a teacher. I am not employed as a teacher and I do not wish to be a teacher. I am employed as a lecturer and in my naïvety I thought my job was to know my 'field', contribute to it by research, and to lecture in my specialism.[7]

The distinction between lecturing and teaching and the emphasis on one's specialism reflects a view of the role of lecturer still widespread particularly in the original university sector. The transition to guide/facilitator of learning implies a change of emphasis from that based predominantly on subject knowledge or curriculum content to an equal emphasis on the process skills involved in supporting learning and probably to a greater emphasis on competences. It significantly changes what is required of an effective lecturer. As yet there is inadequate acknowledgement of this change and its consequences at senior levels in many institutions. There is, of course, now an increasing emphasis on pedagogic skills and teaching competence by many university managements. Yet ambivalence still exists within the system, and there is a frank acknowledgement that most reward systems do not reflect such changes. Audit and assessment reports regularly highlight the discrepancies between the formal objectives of universities and academic departments and the day-to-day experience of lecturers.

> Teaching performance did not appear to be widely perceived by members of staff whom the audit team met as playing a major role in determining promotion. Both senior and junior staff representing several

departments told the audit team that research, and specifically publications, was felt to be of paramount importance.[8]

As in many other universities, until recently research has attracted more recognition and resources than teaching related activities. Initiatives to change this balance are now being introduced, but there are indications that some of the university-wide staff development programmes elicit rather less enthusiasm from teaching staff than do their subject activities.[9]

Knowledge to competences

The traditional view of higher education has always seen knowledge as essentially problematic. Indeed the *raison d'être* underpinning many university curricula has been to steer students away from the more determined world of answers and towards a greater understanding of the essentially questioning nature of knowledge. This has perhaps been particularly dominant in the Arts, Humanities and Social Sciences but other discipline areas have also adopted this kind of approach. Modularity and credit-based systems can appear to restrict such possibilities; inevitably courses are more tightly prescribed as external forces impact upon the way knowledge is organized and packaged.

Learning outcomes must increasingly be specified and skills and competences identified. Some of the first quality assessment reports to be published demonstrate clearly how sharply these challenges are now being posed within universities.

> The assessors noted the lack of emphasis in the [course] aims and objectives on general transferable skills, which had not been integrated into teaching practices in any systematic fashion.[10]

A paper presented to a recent (internal) seminar on the changing nature of higher education at Sheffield Hallam University pointed out that:

> New ways of assessing learning via output measures based on competences point towards new ways of looking at the needs of students. Students should be seen as learners rather than the taught, with the teacher increasingly acting as facilitator rather than lecturer.[11]

This view reinforces the more radical interpretation of the changes now taking place which are affecting the lecturer's role.

More significantly the increasing awareness of the academic interface with National Vocational Qualifications, particularly for those areas of the university curriculum which are vocationally orientated, is posing new challenges. Factors which universities now have to consider are the following:

- Continuing Government commitment to NVQs and GNVQs with concomitant funding arrangements.

- The intention to extend GNVQ to Levels 4 and 5 and the increasing acceptance by universities that GNVQ Level 3 (the so-called vocational A Levels) will become a standard qualification for university entrance.
- Increased emphasis on learning outcomes in curriculum design and as a basis for quality assurance, and a renewed emphasis on competence approaches by employers for in-company training.
- Whether to become accredited providers of, and assessment centres for, GNVQs/NVQs and the implications of so doing.

The challenge will lie in integrating competence approaches with the traditional curriculum and in particular resolving vexed questions as to the equivalence of levels. New tensions with assessment will arise; again there will be staff ill-equipped to meet these new demands without substantial additional support.

Institutional responses to change

Lecturers are also affected, of course, by other changes occurring within the university sector which impact upon their role and perceptions of the academic profession. Some changes, such as the increasing use of fixed-term contracts, have made employment patterns considerably less secure for many new entrants.[12]

There has also been a rapid expansion in the employment of teaching assistants[13] and/or part-time staff.[14] At the margins such a practice has always existed; now it is being systematized and developed as a distinctive segment of the academic labour force with the strategic plans of many institutions setting targets or guidelines for their employment. The University of Edinburgh, for example, plans

> to raise the proportion of fixed term appointments, increase the use of part-time teaching assistants and, where relevant, make use of retraining and redeployment.[15]

While some academic roles are being diversified as a result of the changes outlined in this chapter others are simultaneously becoming more sharply differentiated as the consequences of the 1993 research assessment exercise take effect together with the continuing trend to greater research selectivity.[16] Recent demands for increased accountability for recurrent research funding will only strengthen such differentiation.[17] The widespread formation of graduate schools and research institutes increasingly impacts on the roles of those academics identified as generating research income whether via the funding or the research councils.

The increasing differentiation between higher education institutions or even between departments within institutions, may be reflected in a parallel divergence in academic roles. In future career patterns may be more sharply delineated; the consequences for academic life – not to mention common purpose – have yet to be assessed. Most institutions seem to lack a systematic view of the implications of such changes for academic career patterns or how to support academic career development. They are ambivalent as to what is to be demanded. The danger must be that individual academics find themselves, almost accidentally, allocated roles which lead to constant mismatch of academic interest and expertise and institutional requirements. This danger is all the greater when many institutions, particularly in the traditional university sector, have had a relatively static academic labour force and little opportunity for new recruitment. A high proportion of present academics will have been recruited some 20 to 30 years ago when the world of higher education, the students it recruited, the range of courses offered and the expectations of academics were very different. Much of the change, particularly over the last decade, has not been the result of open national debate and consideration about the role of higher education. Rather a decision was taken to use funding strategies (including bidding for funds) to introduce a strong competitive element thereby forcing institutions to clarify their institutional mission more sharply. Concentration of research funding simply provides a further overlay. Institutions now openly position themselves in the higher education 'marketplace'. A recent seminar at one university noted that:

> Some former polytechnics have decided not to compete for funded research, preferring to act as feeders to others where research can be undertaken; some are primarily local in character with few aspirations to a serious national role, far less an international one which is one of the hallmarks of the traditional universities.[18]

The consequences for lecturers employed at universities which define, or even more importantly *redefine* their institutional mission is profound. A world of institutional and departmental rankings based on research and publications typical of the original university sector has given way to a more ill-defined and confused set of institutional and departmental reputations. The new types of courses and teaching strategies, often seen as the hallmarks of the new university sector, are increasingly being adopted more widely. Lecturers, often having limited room for manoeuvre, find themselves caught up in the backwash of change of which they frequently have a poor understanding and which they have fewer opportunities to influence.

One thing is certain; professional, including pedagogic, training must be taken more seriously. Erosion of professional autonomy (as lecturers perceive it), and more limited opportunity to teach on courses which mesh with personal academic aspirations, only compound the stress which lecturers are ill-equipped to meet.[19] There appear to be few attempts at effective corporate strategies to meet this challenge. Induction and training is often targeted at individuals rather than academic groups or course teams. Moreover, when role confusion is endemic, induction and training become more difficult to deliver. Institutions urgently need better definitions – even job description! – of lecturers.

Loss and identity

Two things are apparent from the recurrent themes identified by most contributors in writing of the changes in the system. The first is the resonance which the phrase 'academic intimacy' has engendered and how frequently it is picked up in the chapters. Secondly the metaphor of bereavement and loss (of identity) is utilized repeatedly when analysing the cause of low morale amongst many academics. This is a shared diagnosis although few contributors have carried forward this metaphor in formulating ideas for the future.

The literature on bereavement and mourning suggests it is not a unilinear process but rather is cyclical.[20] There is a need to let go of the past and past relationships, have a space for grieving and mourning and yet retain what is positive to build into the present and future if a process of healing or 'reconciliation' is to take place. For some (younger?) academics this might involve building new relationships (directions? courses and structures? styles of teaching?) while for others the ability to incorporate elements of the past while adapting to the present may be sufficient. We are after all talking about human behaviour; yet the prescriptions for recapturing a sense of common purpose or designing a new corporate compact seem to jettison the metaphor which is used so readily when diagnosing the ills of the present.

It is interesting to speculate why this should be so. Is it because it is uncomfortable? It is certainly profoundly unfashionable. But the genesis of the problems which have led to the plea for a renewal of common purpose is at least in part rooted in this human response to loss of professional identity.

Of course there are difficulties with the metaphor since the process of educational change has no agreed diagnosis of 'death' or a definitive moment when 'death' or 'transition' occurs. Should academics fight to restore life or make the transition to a new system? Moreover, there is currently a very foreshortened view of 'the past' as far as academe is concerned. In addition, the external (political) environment, which institutional managements can only neutralize to a limited degree, is profoundly unsupportive of positive transitions because of the symbolic confusions it engenders. Enterprise in higher education, responsiveness, access, accountability – the images they conjure up are positive but the reality, for many, has been a negative experience.

There is also evidence to suggest that in the last decade it has been managers and management groups who have on the whole felt excited and energized by possibilities in the new system even when they have been overtaken by bouts of anxiety or frustration with the difficulties of managing. Nonetheless they have felt freed, been given opportunities, space to develop ideas, have been socially valued by society and been tangibly rewarded for their efforts (consider the stretch in the pay differentials). By contrast, many academics have felt dispirited, undervalued, diminished in their autonomy and have suffered an increasing lack of empathy for the goals of institutions. It is perhaps not surprising that this lack of empathy is strongest in the former PCFC sector institutions. So many of the educational objectives with which they were identified, and to which many academics were personally committed, have come to fruition in circumstances they did not envisage. Many of the most disenchanted are those who espoused such educational objectives in the past.

But the real dilemma goes much deeper than this. Most lecturers are concerned that the spirit of intellectual curiosity which originally attracted them into academic life is no longer regarded as a sufficient *raison d'être* by the very institutions that are supposed to uphold and protect it and assure the conditions in which it will continue to flourish. A *Times Higher Education Supplement* editorial (7 August 1992) highlighted a similar theme in suggesting 'there is no point institutions being free to manage their resources if they have lost control of the intellectual agenda'.[21] In the desire to repackage knowledge in ways which make the product easier to sell or assimilate, the managerial encroachment on to the curriculum can lead into very dangerous waters. When Scott lamented the chronic failure to appreciate the importance of academic autonomy – he was writing in that context of Government policy – he could equally have referred to the ways in which many institutional managements have responded to pressures. The mounting plethora of controls and assessments exemplify the way in which the thrust of this policy has been carried forward within institutions. Academic managers, themselves under pressure to demonstrate institutional accountability, have often failed to protect the internal autonomy of academic staff while ensuring academic accountability.

Facing the future

In the last decade, the focus of much institutional management has been on managing finance, property, industrial relations systems and external relations; the curriculum which should have been at the heart of institutional life was often overlooked. What must now be feared, is the importation of inappropriate managerial styles and processes into the arena of curriculum management. There has to be an understanding of what is at stake and new approaches to the management of change. The curriculum must, above all, be managed differently. Lecturers need to redefine their roles in ways with which they feel comfortable and which are consistent with their responsibilities not only to institutions but also to wider professional and educational bodies including subject associations. It is for this reason too that some new consensus needs to emerge across the HE sector, otherwise academics will continually experience a conflict of loyalties which is exhausting in itself and ultimately unproductive.

There will probably be a permanent and inherent tension for the foreseeable future, between the mission and objectives of institutions and the values and aspirations of academic staff. Those tensions can either be a constructive force underpinning change in the curriculum or a permanent and ultimately destructive source of academic dissatisfaction and low morale. Balancing such tension is probably the key issue in the successful management of curriculum change.

Notes

1. 'The Teaching and Learning Technology Programme' originally UFC Circular 19/92 August 1992 and subsequently Phase 2 HEFCE Circular 30/93 August 1993.
2. Scott, P. (1993) Credit systems and the challenge to academic values and institutional cultures. HEQC CATS Development Project, London.
3. Robertson D. (1993) Flexibility and mobility in Further and Higher Education: Policy Continuity and Progress. *Journal of Further and Higher Education*, 17(1), Spring.
4. Richards, B. (1993) Leader in *The Times Higher Education Supplement*, August 20.
5. University of Leicester, History, HEFCE Quality Assessment Report Q3/93 27–9 April 1993.
6. Robertson, op cit.
7. *The Education Guardian*, 20 September, 1990.
8. University of Edinburgh Quality Audit Report, March 1993. HEQC, Division of Quality Audit, University of Birmingham.
9. University of Essex, Law, HEFCE Quality Assessment Report Q5/93, 27–9 April 1993.
10. University of Manchester, History, HEFCE Quality Assessment Report Q10/93, 4–6 May 1993.
11. Seminar paper, *The Changing Nature of Higher Education*, Sheffield Hallam University, July 1993.
12. See *Universities Statistical Record*, Vol. 3, 1990–1, Table 15, p. 65 'Sources of finance of full-time academic staff'. It should be noted that the *SR* identifies these as 'staff not wholly university funded', the vast majority of whom are on fixed contracts.
13. One indication of the increase is the project at Warwick University, funded under the (former) UFC programmes to encourage flexibility in course provision, 'Training of Teaching Assistants and Graduate Student Teachers'. UFC Circular 17/92.
14. See 'Losing Out: a study of part-time lecturers in New Universities', NAFTHE 1993, and 'Part Time, Poor Deal; a survey of part-time staff in traditional universities', AUT, 1993.
15. Audit Report, University of Edinburgh, loc. cit.
16. Research Assessment Exercise 1992: The Outcome. UFC Circular 26/92.
17. Accountability for Research Funds CP4/93. HEFCE, March 1993.
18. Seminar paper, Sheffield Hallam University, loc. cit.
19. The Quality Audit Report for Lancaster University notes (paragraph 46) that 'the most popular (staff development) courses are those in time management and stress management'.
20. Pincus, L. (1976) *Death and the Family. The Importance of Mourning*. Faber and Faber, London.
21. Leader, *The Times Higher Education Supplement*, 7 August 1992.

Part 4

Facing the Future

9

Common Cause: Prospects for Renewal

Jean Bocock and David Watson

In this chapter we consider the consequences of many of the themes raised in the earlier chapters and their implications for a renewal of common cause. There have been those who have challenged both editors and contributors to this book with the charge of latter-day romanticism. Academic intimacy, common cause, restoring professional identity – are these not relics of a collegial past in which common academic values underpinned the infrastructure and organizational forms of university life? In the view of such critics, common cause appears to look backwards; it is a yearning for the reconstruction of shared values and their organizational reflection which can never be re-created in a post-modern world.

If this charge is to be answered satisfactorily it is essential to identify what basis might underpin common cause in the future, and to establish whether it will provide sufficient strength and durability to help overcome the challenges now facing the world of higher education. Is common cause a realistic or even a reasonable aspiration to have on the part of those who work in late twentieth-century universities?

Managing change in universities

The first section of this book documented the changes which have affected universities in recent years. Middlehurst and Barnett (Chapter 3) set their analysis of the transformation of subject/discipline areas in the context of the wider shifts in the relationships between the state, society and higher education which fundamentally affect the mission universities are expected to fulfil. Scott and Watson (Chapters 1 and 2), identifying ways in which universities have become more highly differentiated, internally as well as externally, acknowledge they are now more complex to organize and manage having embarked upon multiple missions. Sometimes their 'core' businesses have become more difficult to define. Management structures, too, are changing. Initially in transition from collegial to a managerial culture there may be a further phase as differentiation of institutions gathers pace. A third 'post-Fordist' structure may emerge which flattens institutional hierarchies – a transition from a managerial to a strategic culture. This pattern, it is suggested, is more typical of the way many successful private corporations are now managed, particularly those in knowledge-intensive industries. This transition may also give back to faculties, departments, units and even individuals the power they lost in the earlier move from collegial to managerial structures.

These points mirror in interesting ways several recent analyses of managing change in successful private companies. Writers in this school similarly stress the importance of common vision or cause. Senge, for example, urges the importance of building shared vision; Goold and Campbell pinpoint the energy released by common purpose in successful companies, and Cleveland has suggested that collegial, not command, structures have become the more natural basis for organizations in which knowledge workers are the key personnel.[1]

It is worthwhile reflecting on these points in more detail in our consideration of common cause in universities. For Goold and Campbell the most important distinctions between companies concern how and where the centre exercises its influence. They identify three major management styles, current in successful UK companies: strategic planning; strategic control; and financial control. Their account of strategic planning companies and their management styles should seem familiar to many in the world of higher education.

> Strategic planning companies stress the need for co-operation throughout the company to achieve certain key shared purposes; and for long-term strategies to achieve success in an unpredictable, rapidly changing and highly competitive world . . .[2]

As the planning director of one 'strategic planning' company put it:

> For strategic management to succeed there needs to be an openness of style, so there will be free flowing of views at all levels in the organization, and not the typical hide-and-seek of ideas between businesses and the centre.
>   In strategic planning and strategic control companies there is therefore a need to work at building mutual respect. Much depends on tone, symbol and signals, which can often be overlooked in processes that focus more on the content of decisions.[3]

Senge advocates the importance of creating learning organizations, if companies and their employees are to surmount and survive the challenges facing them. You cannot have a learning organization, he asserts, without shared vision. Shared vision fosters risk-taking and experimentation; it changes people's relationships with the organization and the tasks they undertake so they become fully integrated. He also advocates team learning, because 'teams, not individuals, are the fundamental learning unit in modern organizations'. He notes:

> the discipline of team learning starts with 'dialogue', the capacity of members of a team to suspend assumptions and enter into a genuine 'thinking together'. Dialogue can only occur when a group of people see each other as colleagues. Colleagueship does not mean you need to agree or share the same views. On the contrary, the real power of seeing each other as colleagues comes into play when there are differences of view. Choosing to view 'adversaries' as 'colleagues with a different view' has the greater benefits.[4]

Many of the management dilemmas facing higher education therefore appear similar to those described in major industrial companies. This sense of familiarity may be enhanced when we consider the case of other public sector organizations. Osborne and Gaebler, in their recent account of transformations in public service organizations (which they claim to be part of a global revolution affecting all major industrial societies to a greater or lesser degree), advocate the emergence of 'entrepreneurial government'.

> Most entrepreneurial governments promote *competition* between service providers. They *empower* citizens . . . They measure the performance of their agencies, focussing not on inputs but on *outcomes*. They are driven by their goals – their missions . . . They redefine their clients as *customers* and offer them choices – between schools, training programmes . . . They put their energies into *earning* money, not simply spending it, . . . They prefer *market* mechanisms to bureaucratic mechanisms.[5]

While this analysis primarily documents the US public sector experience, many of these features will be easily recognized by observers of the UK scene. Higher education has experienced the effects of similar governmental changes introduced in the last decade, in particular competition, accountability and a customer service ethos.

If we accept that dilemmas facing higher education are therefore often shared with major industrial companies, the literature does not suggest a search for common cause is simply a further, perverse example of academic reluctance to adapt to changed circumstances. It does, however, underline the unprecedented degree of challenge facing all public sector or service organizations and its propensity to inhibit university management and academic staff in the search for common cause and the dialogue necessary to review and rekindle its possible sources in late twentieth-century circumstances.

New stakeholders

A major aspect of the challenge is highlighted in the quotation from Osborne and Gaebler above. The greater acknowledgement of other groups with a legitimate interest in the activities of universities, and the curriculum in particular, has been a marked feature of the recent changes. Most symbolically incorporated in the Students' Charter, which sets out the entitlements of students entering higher education, this identification of other stakeholders has been a key development in the pressures for curriculum change and reform.[6] Not only is an increasingly diverse range of students taking a more active role in shaping courses, and professional and employer perspectives being reflected in curriculum design and content, but managers have the task of mediating these sometimes conflicting pressures. As Middlehurst and Barnett point out, the range of stakeholders is now so diverse that the management of communication systems, particularly with external groups, has become a specialized management task frequently divorced from the day-to-day activities of academics. This can, as they acknowledge, hinder the ability of academics to appreciate the diverse sources of pressures for change and to ascribe the difficulties (as they see it) to arbitrary management decisions or their inability to successfully handle pressures from external sources. Indeed, as Scott and Watson point out, changes in curriculum design and delivery have created a much wider grouping of staff within institutions having a legitimate and increasingly recognized role in the curriculum.

Whether the intimacy of the curriculum can therefore be sustained in the larger and more heterogeneous institutions which universities have become is a key question yet to be resolved. If not, the value systems which have sustained such intimacy – and which were legitimated even by those who did not directly share them – will also fragment, further undermining the basis for common cause.

However as Scott and Watson go on to argue, the idea of intimacy can be sustained in a system which has lost its producer dominance and become more sensitive to other stakeholders. It is not inevitable that the move to a more heterogeneous system will require the replacement of one 'intimate' curriculum model by a wholly formal and externalized system. The difficulty at present is that the debate around the curriculum is diverted by the specific problems of modularization and CATS deflecting the open-ended analysis of models appropriate to the end of the century. In contrast with the current national debate over the future of the school curriculum, in which other stakeholders' views have not only been invited but assiduously courted, there is no widespread debate about the university curriculum. This is particularly curious in the light of the increasing moves to make the various stakeholders – students, parents, employers – make a greater financial contribution. Sooner or later the resulting consumers are going to question what they are being asked to buy, particularly in a society where there has been no automatic assumption of entry to higher education for widespread sections of the community; a state of affairs which, as demonstrated in Chapter 1 has not greatly changed, despite the increase in student numbers.

The curriculum as a source of renewal

We have not fully justified our claim that the curriculum is a source of renewal of common cause. Despite the necessary concessions to interests which steer it in the direction of externally driven instrumentalities ('professional' requirements, 'transferable skills', even 'enterprise') we remain committed to that set of academic values which makes the curriculum a profoundly democratic area of activity. In devising its detail and content presumptions of superiority on the basis of seniority or other standing within the institution fall. Questions of content are settled by argument between equals for this purpose and on merit. All contributors are members of an academic peer group.

In this special sense, common cause lies at the heart of the academic community, and, if the curriculum is to be more effectively managed (as we have argued throughout it should be), the point needs to be reaffirmed by practice. It is entirely consistent with our other major argument: that the scope of the relevant peer group must now be more broadly defined, including new participants from within and without the institution.

There are academics who are excited and fearful in equal measure at the changes now occurring. Just as wider participation is a cause for both celebration and concern, there is a deep ambivalence displayed towards curriculum change which promises both liberation and loss. Without more security as to the ultimate objectives many are reluctant to embark on the journey or start out with reluctance always looking for the earliest stopping point. Many lecturers display profound unease about the extent to which the university is committed to their underlying professional values. Will new stakeholders' interests always prevail at their expense? Will greater accountability to the university for their curricular contributions also recognize their wider accountability to professional peer groups and subject associations?

In reality the university curriculum was never so much a secret garden as a private garden, to which individuals were admitted to appreciate and discuss the topography. If this particular sense of privacy can no longer be sustained in a curriculum which has to be replicable (sometimes literally so with repeat modules) then some assurance must be forthcoming about the importance attached to the personal element in contributions to the curriculum made by individual academics. A new balance will need to be achieved between accountability and privacy. The achievement of that balance requires joint determination between managements and academics with both parties recognizing the importance of the issues at stake. This is only one, albeit important, example of the need for new and jointly agreed boundaries which will help to redefine and clarify areas of autonomy in curricular practice.

Difficulties may arise because the 'rediscovery' of the curriculum on the part of many institutional managements seems largely the consequence of a response to external pressures for change like the spread of modularization and the proposals to change the structure of the academic year.[7]

But as Middlehurst and Barnett make clear, changes in the curriculum are not only the result of institutional responses to external events (e.g. new sources of student recruitment); they also reflect internal intellectual challenges to established social assumptions about the organization of knowledge. If the creation, support and dissemination of knowledge is one of the prime functions of a university then an acknowledgement that the challenges universities face lie as much in the internal dynamics of change within academic disciplines and cultures as in external or extraneous forces, should strengthen the conclusion that common cause will not be found by slavish reference to the past.

It is of course convenient for the academic community to externalize sources of change (and threat) and to fail to acknowledge the extent to which some of the challenges lie within their inner domains or heartland. Yet, paradoxically, such an acknowledgement might provide the foundation for a more balanced view of the future. Indeed one of the prerequisites for a successful transition to a more stable future might be a stringent debate about the causes of present dissatisfaction within the world of higher education, an analysis of the sources of change, and a dialogue about viable organizational and intellectual forms for a future university community. There is of course unlikely to be easy consensus on such highly contentious issues when so many private and public values are seen to be at stake. However, the absence of such self-reflection and dialogue at institutional and system level renders the prospects for a successful transition to a new kind of higher education system less certain. Rational analysis and constructive debate would be both an antidote to the strong feelings which surface when current developments in higher education are discussed and a means of structuring such responses in order to generate a more productive understanding for the future.

There is an urgent need for individuals to locate their own experiences in the wider spectrum of change now affecting higher education. Understanding may not lead to acceptance (although it might lead to greater tolerance); however, there is unlikely to be acceptance without greater understanding. It is too often assumed that those who work in a particular occupation or profession best understand the changes which are influencing or reshaping it. Experience suggests this is far from the case. The academic community, above all, should have a vested interest in the attempt to clarify what has actually changed and to reflect upon whether such change gives cause for fundamental concern. Such a recommendation may seem anodyne or even banal, or even a typical academic response. Yet academics should be committed to careful analysis and diagnosis, and a lowering of the temperature might well result. There have been few genuinely dispassionate analyses of these problems; rather most have been offered by proponents or opponents of one form of organizational change or another. Understanding might be the first step on the road to restoring some of the diminution of professional autonomy which is the cause of so much disaffection.

Implications for action

Understanding and action are, of course, different things. As we have composed this chapter together we have become aware of the different emphases we would each place on suggestions about future action, arising from our most immediate present experience and concerns. Lecturers and managers often face each other nervously, almost willing the other side to make the first move, if only to clarify the competing perspectives through confrontation.

To move from understanding to action involves risk. Many prefer the comfort of existing stereotypes to the uncertainty involved in suspending assumptions, acknowledging the priorities and concerns of others and thereby contributing to a new set of professional judgements. Senge summarizes this process as 'dialogue':

> The discipline of team learning starts with 'dialogue', the capacity of members of a team to suspend assumptions and enter into a genuine 'thinking together'. To the Greeks *Dia-logos* meant a free-flowing of meaning through a group, allowing the group to discover insight not attainable individually.[8]

There are several ways in which the risk can be minimized. Opening up the debate about the curriculum within the university is one. It is important that messages and intentions are understood, which means getting the tone, the symbols and the signals right, as well as the terms. The temperature raised by the whole debate about the current condition of higher education and future prospects has been made more feverish by an injudicious use of slogans and of coded terms. 'Mass higher education' is a good example. For some it implies a principled commitment to wider participation; to others it suggests 'piling them high and teaching them cheap'. Unpacking the concept is an obligation which everyone who uses it must accept.

In our view 'mass higher education' does not imply a revocation of entry standards; rather a broader and more flexible approach to what counts as evidence of 'ability to benefit'. Nor does the term inevitably prescribe new shorter (and cheaper) courses designed to give a diluted taste of higher education to a new mass market; rather, that accelerated routes to established qualifications may make sense for some students with particular intellectual qualities or personal circumstances. It does not mean 'giving up' or 'letting go' of levels of resources below which the quality of the product cannot be guaranteed; rather resistance to rationing access to that product solely on the basis of historical assumptions about what it should cost. Most important of all, use of the term 'mass higher education' does not mean adopting the continental European model of high participation but low completion; the retention and qualification rates of UK higher education have been maintained through the past decade of rapid expansion and maintaining and improving them should remain a goal for the future.

Maintaining professionalism

If there is a single motif to capture desirable as opposed to corrosive reactions to change it probably centres on the concept of professionalism, with all that it implies for mutual respect, cooperation and security. The tasks are changing, the roles are becoming more complex and demanding, and the range of legitimate and valuable career paths increasing. There is an air of amateurism about the efforts of many universities to clarify the staffing consequences of current educational change and to face up to the revision and validation of models of professional behaviour for managers, lecturers and other professional staff.

Professional roles must also be more precisely and creatively defined. 'Lecturing', for example, has been treated in an extraordinarily undifferentiated way. Lecturers have been assumed to be the sole judges – subject only to the periodic scrutiny of their peers (through 'validation' or the like) – not only, of course, of content but also of curriculum delivery and assessment. While strongly prepared for the former task most were, and remain, untrained and ill-prepared for the latter. This situation is improving rapidly, but many members of the academic community are still not optimally prepared to adapt curriculum delivery and assessment to the needs of much higher and more diverse student intakes. Moreover, many of the educational changes which excite controversy impact directly on those areas in which academics experience the greatest professional insecurity (educational technology is another such area).

Lecturers might be more willing to surrender autonomy in these domains if the professional skills required were more clearly elaborated, and they were guaranteed the means to acquire them. If a greater diversity of roles and career paths is to be the pattern in the future, then new professional boundaries must be defined which explicitly retain core values. Greater security is a prerequisite for common cause.

The same is true for managers, who in some special ways have borne the brunt of system-wide policy changes and only short-term resource guarantees. Too often they have been not only the bearers of difficult messages to the academic community but also deemed responsible for the content. As universities become more diverse internally, and more differentiated one from another, it is hardly surprising that management styles and strategies vary. History has also played its part, for example in the 'new' universities as a result of incorporation under the Education Act of 1988. Despite attempts to identify and promulgate 'best' management practice and structures (as seen in the waves of reorganization within the higher education corporations as well as in response to the Jarrett Report) no single model has achieved dominance. We have drawn upon the business management world to suggest that the search for a universal management style is chimerical.

We have also emphasized the particular difficulties in aligning the value systems of universities with effective management structures. In setting out alternative futures (especially in Chapters 2 and 3), we have made clear our preference for a model in which the life of the university is bound up in its curriculum and in which the responsibilities of managers as well as of other groups of staff is to support and develop that curriculum. Making common cause in this way requires commitment to continuous improvement, mutual respect and creativity, as well as a reassertion of professional values for all of the parties concerned.

Notes

1. Cleveland, H. (1985) *The Knowledge Executive.* E.P. Denton, New York. Goold, M. and Campbell, A. (1987) *Strategies and Styles: The Role of the Centre in Managing Diversified Corporations.* Blackwell, Oxford. Senge, P.M. (1992) *The Fifth Discipline: The Art and Practice of the Learning Organization.* Random House, London.
2. Goold, M. and Campbell, A. op. cit., p. 297.
3. Ibid., pp. 303, 305.
4. Senge, P. op. cit., pp. 10, 245.
5. Osborne, D. and Gaebler, T. (1992) *Reinventing Government: How the Entrepreneurial Spirit is Transforming the Public Sector,* pp. 19–20. Addison-Wesley, Wokingham.
6. Department for Education (1993) *Higher Quality and Choice: The Charter For Higher Education.* DfE, London.
7. Higher Education Funding Council for England (1993) *The Review of the Academic Year: A Report of the Committee of Enquiry into the Organisation of the Academic Year.* HEFCE, Bristol.
8. Senge, P. op. cit., p. 10.

Index

The Society for Research into Higher Education

The Society for Research into Higher Education exists to stimulate and co-ordinate research into all aspects of higher education. It aims to improve the quality of higher education through the encouragement of debate and publication on issues of policy, on the organization and management of higher education institutions, and on the curriculum and teaching methods.

The Society's income is derived from subscriptions, sales of its books and journals, conference fees and grants. It receives no subsidies, and is wholly independent. Its individual members include teachers, researchers, managers and students. Its corporate members are institutions of higher education, research institutes, professional, industrial and governmental bodies. Members are not only from the UK, but from elsewhere in Europe, from America, Canada and Australasia, and it regards its international work as amongst its most important activities.

Under the imprint *SRHE & Open University Press*, the Society is a specialist publisher of research, having some 45 titles in print. The Editorial Board of the Society's Imprint seeks authoritative research or study in the above fields. It offers competitive royalties, a highly recognizable format in both hardback and paperback and the world-wide reputation of the Open University Press.

The Society also publishes *Studies in Higher Education* (three times a year), which is mainly concerned with academic issues, *Higher Education Quarterly* (formerly *Universities Quarterly*), mainly concerned with policy issues, *Research into Higher Education Abstracts* (three times a year), and *SRHE News* (four times a year).

The Society holds a major annual conference in December, jointly with an institution of higher education. In 1991, the topic was 'Research and Higher Education in Europe', with the University of Leicester. In 1992, it was 'Learning to Effect' with Nottingham Trent University, and in 1993, 'Governments and the Higher Education Curriculum: Evolving Partnerships' at the University of Sussex in Brighton. Future conferences include in 1994, 'The Student Experience' at the University of York.

The Society's committees, study groups and branches are run by the members. The groups at present include:

Teacher Education Study Group
Continuing Education Group
Staff Development Group
Excellence in Teaching and Learning

Benefits to members

Individual

Individual members receive:

- *SRHE News*, the Society's publications list, conference details and other material included in mailings.
- Greatly reduced rates for *Studies in Higher Education* and *Higher Education Quarterly*.
- A 35% discount on all Open University Press & SRHE publications.
- Free copies of the Precedings – commissioned papers on the theme of the Annual Conference.
- Free copies of *Research into Higher Education Abstracts*.
- Reduced rates for conferences.
- Extensive contacts and scope for facilitating initiatives.
- Reduced reciprocal memberships.

Corporate

Corporate members receive:

- All benefits of individual members, plus
- Free copies of *Studies in Higher Education*.
- Unlimited copies of the Society's publications at reduced rates.
- Special rates for its members, e.g. to the Annual Conference.

Membership details: SRHE, 344–354 Gray's Inn Road, London, WC1X 8BP, UK. Tel: 071 837 7880
Catalogue: SRHE & Open University Press, Celtic Court, 22 Ballmoor, Buckingham MK18 1XW. Tel: (0280) 823388

THE LIMITS OF COMPETENCE
KNOWLEDGE, HIGHER EDUCATION AND SOCIETY

Ronald Barnett

Competence is a term which is making its entrance in the university. How might it be understood at this level? *The Limits of Competence* takes an uncompromising line, providing a sustained critique of the notion of competence as wholly inadequate for higher education.

Currently, we are seeing the displacement of one limited version of competence by another even more limited interpretation. In the older definition – one of academic competence – notions of disciplines, objectivity and truth have been central. In the new version, competence is given an operational twist and is marked out by know-how, competence and skills. In this operationalism, the key question is not 'What do students understand?' but 'What can students do?'

The book develops an alternative view, suggesting that, for our universities, a third and heretical conception of human being is worth considering. Our curricula might, instead, offer an education for life.

Contents

Introduction – Part 1: Knowledge, higher education and society: The learning society? – A certain way of knowing – We are all clerks now – Part 2: The new vocabulary: 'Skills' and 'vocationalism' – 'Competence' and 'outcomes' – 'Capability' and 'enterprise' – Part 3: The lost vocabulary: Understanding Critique – Interdisciplinarity – Wisdom – Part 4: Competence reconsidered: Two rival versions of competence – Beyond competence – Retrospect and coda – Bibliography – Index.

224pp   0 335 19341 2 (Paperback)   0 335 19070 7 (Hardback)

FIRST DEGREE
THE UNDERGRADUATE CURRICULUM

Geoffrey Squires

There are books about every aspect of higher education except the one thing that gives all these their *raison d'être*: the curriculum. *First Degree* describes, for the first time, the overall pattern of undergraduate courses in the UK, and analyses it in terms of theories of knowledge, the socio-economic context of higher education and models of student development, ending with a chapter on current policies. This wide-ranging book will be of interest not only to academics, administrators and students in the British system, but to all those involved in higher education in other countries who are concerned with the two basic questions of the curriculum: what is taught? and what ought to be taught?

Contents
The undergraduate curriculum – The curriculum as knowledge – Curriculum and culture – Curriculum and student development – Curriculum policy – Glossary – Bibliography – Index.

192pp   0 335 09315 9 (Paperback)   0 335 09316 7 (Hardback)